Eating Disorders and Weight Control

Susan Frissell & Paula Harney

Enslow Publishers, Inc.

40 Industrial Road   PO Box 38
Box 398   Aldershot
Berkeley Heights, NJ 07922   Hants GU12 6BP
USA   UK

http://www.enslow.com

Dedication

To mentors Marie Devlin and Len James, with gratitude for encouragement and support.

—Paula K. Harney, LPC

To Professor Marcel Fredericks, Ph.D., who years ago believed in my ability way before I did, thank you for mentoring me.

—Susan Frissell, Ph.D.

Library of Congress Cataloging-in-Publication Data

Frissell, Susan.
    Eating disorders and weight control / Susan Frissell and Paula Harney.
        p. cm. — (Teen issues)
    Includes bibliographical references and index.
    Summary: Discusses weight control, body image, and eating disorders including the social pressures which may cause them; presents information about diet, nutrition, and exercise.
    ISBN 0-89490-919-3
    1. Eating disorders in adolescence—Juvenile literature. 2. Weight loss—Juvenile literature. 3. Body image in adolescence—Juvenile literature. [1. Eating disorders. 2. Weight control. 3. Self-perception.] I. Harney, Paula. II. Title. III. Series.
RJ506.E18F75   1997
616.85'26'00835—dc21   97-12489
                                            CIP
                                            AC

Printed in the United States of America

10 9 8 7 6 5 4

Cover Illustration: © Corel Corporation

Contents

Acknowledgments

It's never possible to mention all those individuals who proved helpful in accomplishing a task such as this. We do, however, wish to take this opportunity to express our sincere gratitude to all those who have contributed, especially those survivors of eating disorders and their families who so graciously consented to be interviewed for this book.

Thanks must also go to the following: Ann Kakacek; Deb Rummel; Mick Torres; and Susan Lee Kaehler, M.D., director of the Eating Disorders Program at St. Mary's Hill Hospital in Milwaukee, Wisconsin; Vivian Meehan, R.N., founder of ANAD, Highland Park, Illinois; Helen B. Axelrood, Ph.D., founder and director of the Weight Care Institute and Counseling Clinic, Evanston, Illinois; Cathy Devlin, CEDS; Jim Curtis; Nancy Thode, and Valerie Staples, ACSW director, HOPE Program, South Bend, Indiana.

Transferring copy from the computer's hard drive to floppy disk would not have been possible without the technical savvy of Theresa Fanning, Alan Gossard, and John Proulx of VMC Behavioral Healthcare Services Employee Assistance Programs, Gurnee, Illinois.

Many of the stories you will read here consist of personal interviews with eating disorder survivors. We've also written about the struggles of those more noted personalities to illustrate that no one is immune from this disorder. A more detailed list of resources is provided in the Bibliography at the end of the book.

1

Problems of the Overweight Teen

Fourteen-year-old Allison was five feet six inches tall and weighed 220 pounds. In junior high, the kids teased her unmercifully about being fat. She withdrew into herself and became a loner. She tried to cut back on the amount she ate but lost no weight. Allison did not know what to do.[1]

Eighteen-year-old Heather was five feet seven inches tall and weighed eighty-five pounds. Her family was alarmed at her skeletal appearance. Heather thought differently. "When I looked in the mirror," she said, "I thought my stomach was huge and my face was fat."[2]

★ ★ ★

Both Heather and Allison believe they are fat. They show the two extremes of teenage weight problems. One is actually overweight, with all the negative image fat has in today's world. On the other hand, Heather is so fearful of becoming overweight, she actually is starving herself. How much teenagers weigh and what they see in the mirror can be major influences on their lives. Knowing the facts about weight and living a healthy life can be a great relief.

The first step is taking a quiz to reveal your attitudes about weight control. (See pages 17–19 for the quiz.) Perhaps if Allison and Heather had had the chance to take this quiz, they would have been more realistic and accepting of the way their bodies actually are.

The Problem of Being an Overweight Teen

The biggest problem for overweight teens is not having to wear size XXX clothes. Nor are heavy teens less healthy than average-size teens. Some experts say that there is very little connection between being overweight and having poor health in teenagers.[3] Indeed, a repeated pattern of weight gain, followed by dieting, followed by weight gain is called "yo-yo" dieting. This may have worse physical and psychological results than keeping a constant weight, even if that weight is a little heavy by today's standards.[4]

The biggest challenge for the overweight teen is coping with the emotional and social reactions to being overweight. Many overweight people have lower self-esteem and feel unworthy of respect. "Heavy teens can tend to be doormats for other kids. They are often taken advantage of in interpersonal relationships," says Deb Rummel, a teacher who works with overweight teens.[5]

Lauri Hargrove, another teacher of heavy teens, sees it this way: "Heavy female teens sometimes are seen as very available and nonthreatening to teen boys. Some boys date these girls just to take advantage of them."[6]

The negative view many people have of those who are overweight is called the "fat stigma." People believe those who are fat got that way because they are greedy and stuff themselves with lots of food. Heavy teens may not be as well liked as average-size teens. This can cause a teen to think badly of himself or herself and can lower the teen's self-esteem (see Chapter 4).

Allison commented on her own experience. "I got heavy in the sixth grade. My friends teased me a lot. So I became very quiet and shy. I'd stare them down, but not say anything back when they put me down." Allison said it really hurt her feelings to be treated this way. Her self-esteem plunged to a low level.

The Physical Result of Being Overweight

The most important physical consequence of obesity for teens is that heavy children often become heavy adults.[7] Although many chubby children lose their "baby fat" and slim down naturally as they grow up, some do not. Allison could easily become an obese adult. This is because her body has excess fat and has become highly efficient in maintaining higher than normal levels of fat. In adults, this can lead to medical problems such as diabetes, heart disease, high blood pressure, and stroke.

Also, more teens are obese now than ever before. In 1963, 15.8 percent of teens ages twelve to seventeen were obese. In 1980, 21.9 percent were obese. One reason for this difference might be because Americans of all ages, including teens, are exercising 10 percent less now than ten years ago.[8]

Accepting Oneself

Today's world may place too much emphasis on thinness. More emphasis should be placed on appreciating people for who they are, not what size they are. But sometimes parents are overly concerned that their child is overweight.

One overweight woman reported, "I went to my first Fat Camp at age five. I was away from home for thirteen weeks. This was because my parents were concerned that I might become overweight.

"Now, I am a large woman. I swim a lot, I have a Ph.D., I'm successful, and happy with my life. Why don't we accept people as they are?"[9]

Many obese teens who heard this woman's story did not believe that she was happy. They thought, "To be happy, a person must be thin." They believed the fat stigma. They believed, "Fat means bad (or lazy, or greedy, or unhappy)."

Why People Are Overweight

To explain why Allison is overweight, scientists would say that she had eaten more calories than her body needed. But what is a calorie?

A calorie is the unit used to measure the energy in food. When a person eats, the digestive system turns the food into energy. The body then uses the energy or stores it as fat. If the energy gets stored as fat often enough, the person becomes obese.

However, it is more complicated than it may seem. Two people can be the same size and eat the same number of calories, and yet one gets fat and the other does not. Sometimes a thin person can eat even more calories than a heavy person yet remain thin. Why does this happen?

Overeating alone rarely causes a person to become overweight. Allison was not bad, weak-willed, greedy, self-indulgent, or lazy . . . any more than anyone else! Obesity is complicated, caused by many forces working together. Those factors include:

▢ Genetics (forces Allison was born with): Parents can pass along to their children the physical conditions in their bodies that make them fat. Forty percent of children of one obese parent will also be obese. And 80 percent of children with two obese parents will be overweight.

▢ Forces that developed during Allison's life: Fat cells can grow bigger. Once they are big, they cannot get small very easily. Also, fat cells can increase in number . . . but they do not decrease very readily. Also, the human body works hard to *keep* fat once it has it. This may be because millions of years ago, humans did not have food readily available. So the body learned to store fat once it was gained to help survive future famine. One expert explains it this way: "Excess weight is a biological problem. When people develop excess weight at any point in their lives, their bodies become especially efficient and effective in maintaining higher than normal levels of fat."[10]

What Causes Obesity?

There are four factors that contribute to obesity:

1. Eating too much
2. Exercising too little
3. Poor eating habits
4. Heredity

Eating too much. This does not necessarily mean eating a lot of food. Many people who are overweight do not stuff themselves with too much food. It does mean eating too much of the wrong kinds of food. If Allison's regular diet included lots of high-fat or high-sugar foods like chocolate, fried foods, potato chips, ice cream, cake, or cookies, she could easily become obese. Fat has more than twice the calories of other food types, such as protein and carbohydrates. Many Americans eat 40 to 50 percent of their daily calories in fat. This is like eating a stick of margarine a day!

A certain number of calories are needed every day just to continue living. More calories are needed to supply energy to work, run, play, and think. To find out how many calories are needed to keep a current weight, a normally active person could multiply that weight by twelve. For example, if the current weight is 124 pounds, multiply 124 by 12, which equals 1,488 calories needed to maintain that weight. An inactive person would multiply by ten, and a very active person would multiply by fifteen.

A pound of weight equals 3,200 calories. So if Allison ate only 450 more calories than she needed every day for a week, she would gain a pound of fat. She could add those calories by eating as little as one extra candy bar or one medium serving of fries a day.

Exercising too little. How many calories Allison eats must be balanced with how many she burns up through activity. If Allison is busy and active, she will use more calories than if she sits and watches a lot of television. American teenagers spend about twenty-two hours a week watching television and playing video games. Some experts have found that watching lots of television can be connected to obesity. Teens who watch lots of television expend less energy and are less physically fit than teens who watch less television. So, it is no surprise that 21 percent of teens, age twelve to nineteen, are overweight.[11]

Exercise is important in weight management because it helps boost the body's metabolism, or how fast the body burns up calories. Remember the example of two people of the same size who eat the same calories but one is overweight and one is not? The difference could be that the thinner person exercised more and used up more calories. Also, the thinner, active person could have developed more muscle, while the overweight person had more fat. Muscles burn more calories, even while resting . . . so the muscular person has a higher metabolism and so is thinner. Two people who are the same size and have the same caloric intake could have different results due to differences in exercise, amounts of muscle/fat, and metabolism.

Poor eating habits. One explanation for the recent increase in obesity is the change in the eating habits of Americans. More people are eating fast food, which is usually high in calories and fat. Fewer people eat while sitting down with their families, sharing conversation and enjoying time together. Instead, more meals are eaten on the run, so food is not eaten slowly and with pleasure. When eating too fast, it is very easy to eat too much. When in a hurry, it is very easy to grab the foods that are quick to pick up, like cookies, chips, or other high-calorie, high-fat snacks.

Marissa is a teen who learned to change her eating habits as part of a healthy weight management program. "I learned that even little things can help. I learned to put my fork down between bites. I learned

Measure Your Body Mass

To be more than 20 percent above the ideal weight is to be obese. What is a person's ideal weight? There is no simple answer. Height and weight tables are available, as is a chart called the "body mass index" or BMI. But no chart has the correct answer for every person. There are many things to consider, such as:

1. Does a person have a small-, medium-, or large-size frame?

2. Is the person a male with more than 25 percent body fat? Or is the person a woman with more than 30 percent body fat?

3. How old is the person? Many charts are based on adult sizes and do not fit teenagers.

Body mass index, or BMI, is the way many experts measure obesity. It is a figure that combines height and weight. To find your BMI, find your correct weight in the left-hand column. Move across the row to the correct height. The number at the top of that column is your BMI.

In general, adolescents with a BMI of 21 to 29 could be at risk for obesity. A BMI of 30 or more could mean obesity.[12] Allison's BMI was 35, for example. In contrast, Heather's was 13. These numbers are meant to be guidelines only, not a magic answer.

Some experts say that overweight means something different from obesity. But because the difference is so small, this book uses the words "overweight" and "obesity" to mean the same thing.

☐ = Not obese ☐ = At risk for obesity ☐ = Possibly obese

	5'0"	5'1"	5'2"	5'3"	5'4"	5'5"	5'6"	5'7"	5'8"	5'9"	5'10"	5'11"	6'0"	6'1"	6'2"
100	20	19	18	18	17	17	16	16	15	15	14	14	14	13	13
105	21	20	19	19	18	18	17	17	16	16	15	15	14	14	14
110	22	21	20	20	19	18	18	17	17	16	16	15	15	15	14
115	23	22	21	20	20	19	19	18	18	17	17	16	16	15	15
120	23	23	22	21	21	20	19	19	18	18	17	17	16	16	15
125	24	24	23	22	22	21	20	20	19	19	18	17	17	17	16
130	25	25	24	23	22	22	21	20	20	19	19	18	18	17	17
135	26	26	25	24	23	23	22	21	21	20	19	19	18	18	17
140	27	27	26	25	24	23	23	22	21	21	20	20	19	19	18
145	28	27	27	26	25	24	23	23	22	21	21	20	20	19	19
150	29	28	28	27	26	25	24	24	23	22	22	21	20	20	19
155	30	29	28	28	27	26	25	24	24	23	22	22	21	21	20
160	31	30	29	28	28	27	26	25	24	24	23	22	22	21	21
165	32	31	30	29	28	28	27	26	25	24	24	23	22	22	21
170	33	32	31	30	30	28	28	27	26	25	25	24	23	23	22
175	34	33	32	31	30	29	28	28	27	26	25	25	24	23	23
180	35	34	33	32	31	30	29	28	27	27	26	25	25	24	23
185	36	35	34	33	32	31	30	29	28	27	27	26	25	24	24
190	37	36	35	34	33	32	31	30	29	28	27	27	26	25	25
195	38	37	36	35	34	33	32	31	30	29	28	27	27	26	25
200	39	38	37	36	34	33	32	31	31	30	29	28	27	27	26
205	40	39	38	36	35	34	33	32	31	30	30	29	28	27	27
210	41	40	39	37	36	35	34	33	32	31	30	30	29	28	27
215	42	41	39	38	37	36	35	34	33	32	31	30	29	28	28
220	43	42	40	39	38	37	36	35	34	33	32	31	30	29	28
225	44	43	42	40	39	38	36	35	34	33	32	32	31	30	29
230	45	44	42	41	40	38	37	36	35	34	33	32	31	30	30
235	46	45	43	42	40	39	38	37	36	35	34	33	32	31	30
240	47	46	44	43	41	40	39	38	37	36	35	34	33	32	31

to substitute healthy food for 'fat' food, like using PAM instead of butter or margarine when I cooked."[13]

Heredity. Deb Rummel, a physical education teacher, tells her obese students, "Take a mental picture of what your overweight Mom and Dad look like. That's where you're headed unless you do something about it."

Scientists are not entirely sure why heredity is so important in weight management. It probably has to do with inherited metabolism, hormone levels, or other factors. Recently scientists discovered something important about a hormone called "leptin." This natural substance appeared to trigger a slimming process when given to obese rats. It appeared to boost energy levels so the rats ate less food. As a result, the obese rats became normal weight.[14] Incorrect levels of leptin in the body may be linked to the inheritance of obesity.

A Physical Management Program at a High School

Healthy weight management practices are important and very possible. Kari is a student in Deb Rummel's Physical Management program at her high school. When she applied what she learned in class, she lost forty pounds in fifteen weeks. "Then I gained it all back," she said. "I tried to change too fast. Also, I was inconsistent; one minute I'd eat a big cheeseburger with bacon, and the next minute I'd eat carrot sticks."[15] We will learn more about Kari's progress in the last chapter.

Physical Management programs were started by Eileen Solberg in Montana several years ago. The class meets for fifty minutes a day, each school day. The program teaches students about healthy weight management practices in an enjoyable way. In this class, Kari learned to set realistic goals, maintain positive attitudes, eat and exercise in healthy ways, and get support from family and friends. She was fortunate to have a weight management program at her high school. Allison was also a member of this class. She lost weight but, more importantly, learned to raise her self-esteem and become more confident.

Teens in Physical Management learn assertiveness skills and work on building their self-esteem so they can overcome the effects of the fat stigma and start to feel good about who they are. "We do a lot of role-playing on how to say 'no' and become assertive," says teacher Deb Rummel. Teens learn to express anger appropriately, so they neither lose their temper nor stuff it all down inside. Physical Management teaches the teens to deal with the emotional and social effects of being overweight as well as to develop healthy weight management practices.

Unhealthy Weight Management Practices

However, many teens try to lose weight in risky, unhealthy ways. Because American culture places great emphasis on thinness (see Chapter 3), many people, like Heather (who weighed only eighty-five pounds but thought she was fat), believe they have to be thin to be happy, attractive, or successful. Some experts believe this can lead to "unhealthy weight-loss practices and can contribute to the development of eating disorders." These experts found that 43.7 percent of the teen girls and 15.2 percent of the teen boys they studied were trying to lose weight.[16] Although some students used safe means to lose weight, others used risky methods such as skipping meals, inducing vomiting, or ingesting diet pills.

In addition, experts have found that depriving oneself of sufficient nutrition and yo-yo dieting may "increase the likelihood of weight gain and obesity in adulthood." Also, unhealthy weight-loss practices may be connected to slowed growth, delayed start of puberty, and impaired social development.[17]

Some unhealthy weight management practices may become an actual eating disorder, a very serious problem that can affect a person's life for many years. Some eating disorders become so severe they lead to death. Several chapters in this book will explain more about eating disorders. Allison and Kari learned to lose weight in healthy ways. On the other hand, Heather developed a severe eating disorder that required hospitalization and years of treatment.

Test Your Weight I.Q.

1. **You get up in the morning, look in the mirror, and say, "I'm so fat!" You say this about a hundred times a day. You are fourteen, are five feet four inches tall, and weigh 120 pounds. You wish you were 110 pounds. You are constantly dieting. You . . .**

   a. are really a blimp in disguise and need to lose weight.

   b. are right on target for your age and height.

   c. probably could stand to lose a few pounds.

2. **You have tried the Grapefruit Diet, Fat-Burning Soup Diet, even the Coke diet. When you get frustrated with one, you start another. You . . .**

   a. may win the prize for "Goofiest Diet of the Year" award but will not lose much weight, or keep it off for very long.

   b. need to pay big bucks to really lose weight, like joining an expensive health club, buying special diet foods, etc.

   c. just have not found the right fad diet and should keep looking.

3. **You are out with the gang and order only a salad and a glass of water. Back home, you beeline for the pantry and wolf down doughnuts when no one is looking. You . . .**

   a. yell at Mom/Dad for buying doughnuts and other fattening stuff. Don't they know you're trying to lose weight?

   b. decide to ask your school counselor to help you figure out why you're uncomfortable eating normally in front of others.

   c. resolve to never eat another doughnut as long as you live.

4. **You were a pudgy kid. Now you have slimmed down, and your parents are bugging you to eat more! They're never satisfied! You . . .**

   a. eat ice cream and french fries to keep your parents off your case.

   b. ignore them.

   c. find a calm moment to discuss your feelings and concerns with your parents.

5. **You get up early to jog for twenty minutes before school. After school, you do an aerobics tape for forty-five minutes. After dinner, you do the real exercise—you run five miles. You . . .**

   a. may be exercising too much.

   b. wish you had time to do more.

   c. get irritated when your parents urge you to slow down.

6. **You talk about how fat you are all the time. Your friends are sick of hearing it. You . . .**

   a. need to lose weight so you will not be fat and will not need to talk about it all the time.

   b. need to find better friends who are more understanding.

   c. need to find out why you talk about being fat so much.

7. **Being thin is VERY important to you. In fact, it is the MOST important thing in your life. If you gained five pounds, you think you would hide out in your room and not eat until you got thin again. You . . .**

   a. need to find out why being thin is so important to you.

   b. are to be congratulated for knowing your priorities.

   c. remind yourself that a person can never be "too thin or too rich."

8. **You hate to exercise. You are the original couch potato. You figure you will lose weight by not eating much, so you skip breakfast and lunch and only eat dinner while lying in front of the TV. You . . .**

   a. can expect to be slim and trim in a short time.

   b. try to get your friends to join your plan.

   c. could use more information on weight management.

9. **Kids at school call you a "Blimp" and "Lardo." It hurts when they laugh at how slow you are in gym class. You . . .**

   a. make sure you have plenty of Ben and Jerry's Chocolate Chunk ice cream at home to soothe your feelings after school.

   b. tell the teasers to shut up.

   c. ask a counselor to help you find a way to laugh at the situation, and maybe learn to tease them back.

10. **You are dieting because you just know you will have a heart attack like grandpa or diabetes like grandma if you are fat like them. You are really afraid of this, so you try to lose weight by fasting (no food, only liquids) two days a week. You . . .**

    a. are right to be concerned, because fat, heart disease, and diabetes can run in families.

    b. are right to be concerned but could use a better weight management plan.

    c. do not need to worry about heart disease or diabetes.

11. **Your doctor said your ideal weight is 125 pounds. You weigh 156 pounds. This is more than 20 percent above your ideal weight. You . . .**

    a. decide to change doctors.

    b. need to ask your doctor to help you develop a healthy plan for weight reduction.

    c. need to start a 900-calorie-per-day diet immediately.

Answers, page 125

2

What Are Eating Disorders?

Estimates are that one of every two hundred females ages ten to thirty years suffers from the serious eating disorder known as anorexia nervosa. Of the three major eating disorders—anorexia nervosa, bulimia nervosa, and binge-eating disorder—anorexia gets the most attention.

Anorexia Nervosa

Anorexia nervosa probably receives more attention than the other eating disorders because it has such appallingly drastic results. The sight of a once-lovely teenager, now skin and bones, looking like a refugee from a concentration camp, is quite shocking. Even more appalling is to hear this person insist that she is "too fat" and needs to lose more weight.

When a person starts sliding into anorexia, she usually has low self-esteem (see Chapter 4). She has a low opinion of her worth as a person. Also, she may have suffered several important losses in her life, such as the death of a loved one. Her life feels out of control. She decides that by controlling her body, either by refusing to eat or exercising excessively, she will feel more in charge of her life and will start to feel better about herself.

In time, a person with anorexia becomes obsessed with food. She may begin to collect cookbooks. She may prepare lavish, gourmet meals for her family but refuse to eat anything herself. One girl would eat only three thin slices of green pepper for lunch. Her whole life, all her thinking, planning, and dreaming, became

Signs of Anorexia

- ☐ Hyperactivity, depression, or moodiness
- ☐ Intense fear of being fat
- ☐ Belief that they are fat even when very thin
- ☐ Constipation and/or loss of menstrual periods
- ☐ Development of fine, downy hair on body
- ☐ Complaints of nausea or bloating after eating small amounts of food
- ☐ Feeling cold much of the time
- ☐ Hair loss

focused on avoiding food and becoming thinner. She never felt she was thin enough, not even when she was skin and bones and close to starvation.

The profile of a "typical" anorexic is that of a young, Caucasian female who is often a high achiever and usually very intelligent. She is self-disciplined and very critical and demanding of herself. In addition, many anorexics feel an intense need to please other people. One expert found that anorexics have a much greater need for approval from others than nonanorexics have. And, although anorexics showed greater conformity and conscientiousness, they showed less sensitivity to their own inner needs than did nonanorexics. In shutting off some feelings, anorexics may have learned to completely ignore their own hunger pangs.[1]

Bulimia Nervosa

Someone with bulimia nervosa feels out of control. However, in addition to the external environment seeming to be out of control, someone with bulimia feels his or her eating habits are out of control as well. A person suffering from bulimia gets into a vicious cycle of

- Feeling stress, or another powerful emotion he or she doesn't know how to handle

- Eating a large quantity of pleasurable food (this is called "bingeing") to distract from the emotional pain

- Feeling terrified that this huge quantity of food will turn into fat

▢ Purging through use of laxatives, diuretics, vomiting, or excessive exercise

▢ Feeling a temporary relief that is soon replaced by guilt, shame, and powerlessness . . . and the cycle begins anew

A teenager with bulimia looks normal. He or she does not become emaciated as does an anorexic. This is because the methods used to lose weight do not work very well. So the disorder may be even more hidden than an anorexic's. The bulimic can continue to function in his or her daily life in a relatively normal way. However, the impact on the person's health is very real. Some recovering bulimics have had to spend up to $10,000 on repairs to their teeth from vomiting. Also, the vomiting upsets the electrolyte balance in the body, which can cause a heart attack and death.

Bulimia may be even more common than anorexia. One study of college freshmen showed that 4 percent of women and .4 percent of men had a history of bulimia.[2]

Some bulimics use laxatives or exercise excessively. Abuse of laxatives can lead to serious dehydration and chemical imbalances in the body. One dramatic example is told by Cherry Boone, daughter of Pat Boone, a famous singer in the 1950s and 1960s.

Cherry relates that one night she and her husband were entertaining friends. She looked her normal, but very thin, self when the evening began. However, she had already swallowed a large amount of laxatives. In three hours, her face became skeletal, with her skin stretched tightly over her skull, her teeth appearing huge when she tried to talk. She shrank to an "awful,

Natalie

I was always tall. All through elementary school, I was the tallest kid in my class. I was also the tallest at home: I have four brothers who are shorter than me! No matter where I went, I felt I never fit in; I was too big. I was ashamed of my height and got teased a lot. My self-esteem was pretty low.

When I got to high school, it was very important to me to always be in control of my life. My grades were perfect because I could control them. I had lots of friends, although I felt phony with them because I was always trying to be who they wanted me to be.

I was a good athlete; again, I could control my achievements.

Then, in my junior year of high school, two events happened that I couldn't control. My best friend was sent to a foster home in another state after I had reported that she was being sexually abused by her stepdad. I had no contact with her for a long time after that. I missed her and blamed myself for her being sent away.

Then, my boyfriend broke up with me. We'd been together for three years. I was devastated. I didn't want to break up, but he insisted.

Also, at that time, I had to start making decisions about colleges and careers. I wasn't ready for this. Everyone else seemed to know what they wanted to do. I still asked people, "What do you think I should do (for a career/college choice)?" Everything was happening too fast. My life felt very out of control.

Somehow I got the idea my weight was something I could control. I began a healthy weight loss diet and began to lose pounds. I also started an exercise program. People complimented me on how good I looked, and I hadn't heard compliments for a while. It felt good to be complimented and be back in control again.

Somewhere, though, I lost control of my dieting and exercising. By the time I started college, I had lost 50 percent of my body weight. I weighed 70 pounds, and I'm 5'11"! I was so weak I couldn't open doors for myself. In order to get into the classroom building, I had to wait for another student to come by and open the door for me. I couldn't carry my backpack! But I never thought it was because I wasn't eating. I thought it was because I was a "wimp." I never thought I was thin enough. In fact, I would wake myself up every hour at night so I could do exercises in bed.

So not only was I starving myself, I was also overexercising. If I ran one mile on Monday, I'd wake up on Tuesday and tell myself, "I have to run one-and-a-half miles today since I ran one mile yesterday." By the end of the week, I'd be running four or five miles a day.

When I started my exercise program, I exercised for three short periods a day. I'd go for a short jog or spend ten minutes on the stationary bike. This wasn't excessive. But by the time I got to college, I was exercising every chance I got—even in bed at night.[3]

(Natalie's story will be continued in Chapter 4.)

Signs of Bulimia

- ❏ Eating lots of high-calorie/high-fat foods that require little preparation
- ❏ Feeling bad about oneself after a binge
- ❏ Feeling ashamed and depressed about eating habits; feeling these habits are out of control
- ❏ Becoming a secret eater/binger
- ❏ Having swollen salivary glands
- ❏ Becoming dependent on laxatives, diuretics, or diet pills
- ❏ Having dental problems caused by acid on teeth
- ❏ Having broken blood vessels in eyes from vomiting

mummy-like figure before everyone's eyes in the course of an evening." She had become drastically dehydrated from the laxatives. Fortunately, Cherry got into treatment and is recovering from bulimia today.[4]

When a person begins the binge-purge cycle, he may be delighted to have found a way to lose weight. He may think that purging is an easy way to eat whatever is wanted and yet not get fat. Purging may seem to be a way to "have your cake and eat it, too."

However, the initial thrill soon wears off. Then the bulimic is left with the self-hate and shame that comes from seeing piles of empty candy wrappers, doughnut boxes, ice-cream cartons, and cookie packages under the bed or feeling the extreme embarrassment Cherry Boone felt when her then-boyfriend caught her binge-ing on greasy leftovers from her dog's food dish.

Treatment can be effective for bulimics as well as anorexics. Chapter 6 will go into more detail about how to find effective help.

Binge-Eating Disorder

Experts know the least about binge-eating disorder. It is like the other eating disorders because it involves feelings of low self-worth, guilt, shame, and powerlessness. It is especially like bulimia because it involves eating large quantities of food in a short period of time. Also like bulimia, a binge eater will use food to soothe or distract himself or herself from painful events or feelings. The person feels his or her life and eating habits are out of control, and becomes obsessed with food.

However, unlike bulimia, someone with binge-eating disorder does not try to purge the food by vomiting or exercising. As a result, someone with this disorder may become overweight. Binge eaters are either normal weight or overweight and may look like someone with simple obesity (see Chapter 1). The difference is that their overweight is caused by compulsive overeating, with heredity and other factors being less important. Binge eaters have all the feelings of guilt and shame and being out of control that people with other eating disorders have. Because this disorder is not as dramatic or life-threatening as anorexia or bulimia, it has been studied less, and so less is known about it. It is estimated that about 2 percent of the population is affected.[5]

Nell

I feel like I've been bulimic my whole life. My entire family is overweight. My mother died of (the medical complications of) bulimia. So food and weight control have always been a big deal in my life.

When I was three years old, my mother got some diet pills, and my whole life changed. She started boiling my hamburgers (instead of frying them)! And we started having D-Zerta for dessert. She got strung out on the pills. Her hair fell out. She vomited food back up. It was not a happy time.

In fourth grade, I began to restrict my food intake. I wouldn't eat my cookie in my school lunch, and I wouldn't eat breakfast. I wanted to lose weight. All my life I heard, "Don't be fat! Don't get 'sugar' [diabetes]! You'll have to fight fat all your life!"

I was twelve or thirteen when the actual bulimia started. Mom had a heart attack, and I had to take care of her while she recuperated. To get away from the problems at home, I'd go for a walk or bike ride for two or three hours a day. I wanted to escape the reality of my family life. I wanted to be totally different from my family. I talked constantly *about being fat. I couldn't carry on a normal conversation with anyone without mentioning how fat I was.*

I stopped eating for awhile. Once, I fasted for two whole weeks, drinking only liquids. I got compliments on how good I looked as I lost weight. This felt wonderful! It was the first time I ever heard compliments on how I looked! I started binge-eating

(eating a lot of food in a short time) and then making myself throw it back up.

When I was fourteen, my mother died. I had to grow up fast. My whole life changed again. But the bulimia stayed the same. When I would go on a date, I'd eat only one french fry. I really believed if I ate more, my date would know I was fat! And it didn't matter if I was a size fifteen or a size nine; I always felt fat. I was never thin enough.

My bulimia continued through my teen years and well into my marriage. I got into rituals, like weighing myself a lot. Sometimes I got on the scales forty times a day. When the bulimia was at its worst, I was throwing up twenty times a day.

When I got pregnant, I stopped throwing up. I was happy to not have to worry about being thin. So I overate. I ate everything I wanted. I ate in binges, and I gained a lot of weight. Of course, after the baby's birth, I started purging again to lose weight.[6]

(The ending to Nell's story will be told in Chapter 6.)

Although most eating disorders start before twenty years of age, many adults thirty, forty, even fifty years old seek help for this problem. Signs of eating disorders can be detected in preteens, as well. So people of any age can develop an eating disorder.

In fact, researchers have found that as young as fourth grade, girls have become overly concerned about their weight. Fifty percent say they diet because they are "too fat." Also, 90 percent of junior and senior high school girls diet, and only 10 percent are actually overweight.[7]

No one tries to get an eating disorder. For many anorexics, the initial weight loss is accidental and comes after an illness or surgery or is due to sadness from an important loss. Others begin with a weight-loss diet that does not stop when the target weight is reached. In fact, some experts believe eating disorders should be called "feeling" disorders. This is because the disordered, or unusual, eating habits are the *result* of a problem of dealing with feelings.

One expert put it this way: "If a person can focus on weight, body size or food, she *doesn't* have to focus on problems that seem unsolvable. She doesn't have to find appropriate problem-solving skills. She has the 'perfect solution' to decrease painful feelings . . . at least temporarily."[8]

Eating disorders are difficult to treat. Early detection and treatment are crucial. The good news is that some 50 percent of anorexics report recovery. The sad news is that people can die from eating disorders. According to different estimates, from 3 percent to 20 percent of people with anorexia nervosa and bulimia die from medical complications of these disorders. This death rate is higher than any other mental disorder.[9]

Eating disorders appear to be increasing in recent years. However, anorexia is not a brand-new illness. In 1874, a researcher named William Full described anorexia nervosa to the London Clinical Society. Anorexia nervosa was also described in literature from the Middle Ages. So, although eating disorders are not new, the fact that so many people have them is new. They appear to occur only in well-fed countries like the United States, Great Britain, and other countries with a high standard of living and abundant food supplies.

Although statistics appear to focus on females, it is important to note that both boys and girls can develop eating disorders. People of all ages, races, and ethnic groups can develop anorexia nervosa, bulimia, or binge-eating disorder. Athletes are often at risk, especially gymnasts, dancers, wrestlers, swimmers, and participants in any sport that emphasizes weight control.

The Nature of Eating Disorders

The symptoms of the three eating disorders can seem confusing. Also confusing is the fact that the same person can have a different disorder at different times of her life. Nell, for example, was mostly bulimic, but during her pregnancy, she quit vomiting. So at that time, she was a binge eater. This type of shift in symptoms happens to many people with eating disorders.

Some experts are studying the chemicals in the human brain to find causes of eating disorders. Important chemicals called serotonin and norepinephrine are found in smaller amounts in people with eating disorders. Depressed people also have small amounts of these brain chemicals. So doctors have found that prescribing antidepressants can help treat eating disorders as well as depression.

A brain hormone called cortisol is found in greater amounts in anorexics. This hormone increases in response to stress. Another brain hormone that increases with stress is vasopressin. This, too, is found in greater amounts in people with eating disorders. Finally, scientists have discovered brain chemical similarities between people with eating disorders and people with a mental disorder called obsessive-compulsive disorder. This may explain the persistent thoughts and ritualistic behaviors that may be part of an eating disorder. As scientists learn more about these complex brain chemicals, they may unlock the secrets of how eating disorders begin and how to help people recover from them.[10]

A Common Problem

It is important to remember that people of all ages, races, ethnic groups, and both sexes can have eating disorders. It is also important to remember that the disordered eating behavior of anorexia, bulimia, and binge eating is only the part that can be seen on the outside. What is more important are the feelings hidden deep inside the person.

Simple obesity is not an eating disorder. If the obesity is complicated by psychological factors, then the person could have binge-eating disorder. So, although Allison (Chapter 1) probably had simple obesity, Heather (Chapter 1), Natalie, and Nell had eating disorders.

Eating "Secrets"

1. When you look in the mirror, you see a fat stomach and humongous hips. But your parents think you're too thin and constantly urge you to eat more. You may . . .

   a. be bulimic.

   b. be anorexic.

   c. need to get someone to help your parents understand how fat you really are.

2. Your friends envy you because you can eat all the greasy fries and burgers you want and still keep a slim figure. They want to know your secret diet. You tell them you don't have one. But you DON'T tell them you vomit after every meal. You may . . .

   a. be bulimic.

   b. be anorexic.

   c. need to get new friends.

3. You're forty pounds overweight. You're sick of being so big. But every time someone calls you "Tubby" or "Lardo," you head for the freezer and gulp down a half-gallon of Ben and Jerry's Chunky Monkey ice cream. This distracts you when you're mad, or sad, or anxious . . . or feeling any strong feeling. You may . . .

   a. be anorexic.

   b. be bulimic.

   c. have binge-eating disorder.

4. Your best friend died last month in a car accident. Your parents don't seem to understand anything; in fact, they're screaming at each other and throwing around the big "D" word (divorce). Your boyfriend just split. Everything seems to be out of your control. You decide one thing you can control is your weight, and you go on a strict 900-calorie diet. You may . . .

a. be headed for bulimia.

b. be headed for anorexia.

c. be headed for binge-eating disorder.

5. You're trying to stay slim, and so you weigh yourself quite frequently. Yesterday you weighed yourself ten times; today, twelve times. You feel elated when your weight is down and depressed when it's up. You may . . .

a. be at risk for developing an eating disorder.

b. be bulimic.

c. be anorexic.

6. You eat a lot of food secretly in your bedroom. Yesterday your mother asked why you had so many empty cartons . . . of ice cream, doughnuts, and Hostess Ho-Hos . . . under your bed. She thought they'd been there for months. You didn't tell her it was only a week's worth of trash. You may . . .

a. need to clean your room more often.

b. be a binge eater.

c. be anorexic.

7. You were really mad because your parents wouldn't let you spend the night at your friend's house. You couldn't tell them how you felt or they'd ground you. You made a beeline for the pantry and ate the whole bag of Double Decadence Chocolate cookies. You do this a lot. You may . . .

a. be anorexic.

b. have binge-eating disorder.

c. be bulimic.

8. You believe in keeping physically fit and staying slim. So you exercise three times a day, including a daily five-mile run. Lately, that doesn't seem to be enough exercise. You are planning to find a way to do more. You may . . .

a. be overly concerned with your weight and fitness.

b. be trying to "run away" from something troublesome in your life.

c. Both of the above.

9. This means "ox hunger" or eating large quantities of food in a short period of time:

a. anorexia

b. bulimia

c. binge-eating disorder

10. This means seeming to lack an appetite for food:

a. anorexia

b. bulimia

c. binge-eating disorder

Answers, page 125

3

Body Image and the Pressure to Be Thin

H ow do people with an eating disorder feel about themselves? We can get an idea from some of the following comments:

> "To be absolutely honest, losing weight is the only thing that's important. I don't know why, but I'd give up anything before that."[1]

—Nicola, age seventeen

> "I am thin, I am happy. That's all that matters for now."

—Karen, age eighteen, 113 pounds

> "I wasn't happy, I was depressed, so I lost a little weight. Someone complimented me on my weight loss. I liked it and decided to do more. Nothing else was working, so I turned off life and began dieting."

—Natalie, age sixteen, five feet eleven inches, 150 pounds

"When vomiting (and thinner), I feel prettier and more feminine. I look in the mirror and compliment myself. It gave me confidence because I was doing something about my weight."

—Erin

"Body image determined self-esteem. No fat, no flab equals no fear, no failure."

—Cherry Boone

"I'm not sure what I look like. Sometimes I see one thing (a fat, ugly person), sometimes another (a thin, pretty person). What's real? I'm not sure what others see. Everything is confusing."

—Anonymous

The Myth of the Ideal Body

According to some researchers, teens with eating disorders have learned to respond to life experiences in an unhealthy way, and this pattern is consistently reinforced by the media's "ideal body."[2] This is particularly true for many women, who become paralyzed by feelings of shame, insecurity, and a fear of rejection. It becomes hard for these women to believe they have assets and are unique human beings.

Research shows that almost all women are ashamed of their bodies. It used to be that adult women and teenage girls were affected the most, but now the shame is seen in girls as young as ten and eleven years old. Society's standard of beauty is an image that many young girls buy into, and it is not far from starvation. A *People* magazine poll conducted in 1996 confirmed that 50 percent of nine-year-old girls have dieted, and 10 percent of the teenagers suffering from eating disorders are boys. One to 4 percent of high school and college girls have either anorexia or bulimia, which has doubled since 1976.[3]

More likely to have negative feelings about their appearance than adults, 45 percent of teenagers, according to the *People* poll, report experiencing unhappiness or dissatisfaction with their appearance one or more times a week. The younger someone is, it seems, the more often that person is dissatisfied about how she looks.[4]

By one estimate, 75 percent of teenage girls, faced with pressure from all directions, resort to dieting. They prefer being thin and are not happy if they think they look fat in what they are wearing. Actress Pamela Anderson Lee of *Baywatch* fame and model Kate Moss are held up as epitomes of the perfect body to aspire to. A desire to be thin has led to an increase in the demand for quick fixes, such as plastic and reconstructive surgery.

Body Image and Self-esteem

When reading the comments made by individuals suffering from an eating disorder, it becomes clear that for many people, body image very much determines self-esteem. And today, the body image to which teens aspire is dictated by the media, TV, movies, and advertisements. Many teens feel that if they are not extremely thin like today's models, they are not attractive. However, society's notion of body image is unrealistic and only reinforces the prejudicial attitude that our culture seems to support.

Kathy Najimy, comedian and actress, sees fat as a feminist issue. "I think it's keeping women so obsessed about how they look," she says, "that it keeps us from running the world." A broad statement, perhaps, but the meaning is clear. Most women believe they must obey a rigid beauty regime. A recent advertisement in *People* magazine for the Fox Broadcasting Company features two photos: one of obese women bathing at the beach, the other of actresses from the popular television show *Melrose Place*. The copy reads: "Cool like them or Cool like us. You are what you watch."

At a time when teenage girls are struggling with self-esteem issues, this is just one example of the message being given: "Being thin means you're cool . . . being fat means you're not." And an even worse message is that a person is a justifiable target of ridicule if she is overweight. If a person is overweight (by society's standards), it is not uncommon for him or her to feel discriminated against. Although for some this feeling may be "imagined," it most often is real. It is not cool to be fat.[5]

There is a relationship between body image and self-esteem, and it varies from person to person. Someone who is highly satisfied with his or her body more often has high self-esteem. Body image, body satisfaction, and self-image are positively related. The fact that a person's self-esteem goes up and down depending on weight, changing dramatically from acceptable to awful, demonstrates that shame may be a dominant theme in a person's body image and self-image.

A young woman may be overheard saying that she is thin because her significant other likes her that way. Being able to control her weight gives her feelings of power and attention. "Being thin causes other women to envy you," says one woman. Perceived positive results accompany being thin, such as gaining an identity along with control. Obesity and self-starvation, or anorexia, are not really about food. Rather, they become a symptom of how someone may feel about himself or herself, others, or his or her environment.

For someone with an eating disorder, disturbance about body image is a serious problem. It occurs when an individual has distorted feelings, thoughts, and perceptions about his or her body. Usually the person's perception is different from his or her actual size, shape, and appearance. Certain body parts may also be perceived as ugly, too fat, or too small, when in fact, they are average for the person's age and height.

Shame and Body Image

Most everyone can think of a time in his or her life when deep shame has been felt. As the experience of feeling ashamed is played back, it is accompanied by a flushed face or a shiver down the spine. The memory may be so painful that a person has to turn away from the image in his or her head. This is the emotion of shame, and it is a powerfully painful and complex feeling.

Although most women in Western culture probably do not have an accurate body image, individuals with eating disorders have a more disturbed view of their bodies. They believe that thinness symbolizes power, independence, and control and that being fat means being weak, dependent, and out of control. For someone with an eating disorder, the body becomes an object to be transformed, a tool to bolster self-esteem. Obsessing about size and weight enables a person to ignore what her body is really feeling. Therefore, the relationship begins between shame and body image, or a person's mental picture of what her body looks like.[6] Often, the person with anorexia defends against feeling shame with perfectionism. For a compulsive overeater, hating her body becomes a way of covering up the shame she feels inside. For those with an eating disorder, shame is a complex feeling. For many, they are ashamed of their bodies (body shame) and what their fat represents (weakness). Compulsive eaters may feel shame over their lack of control over food and the size, shape, and weight of their bodies.

There are three main factors that influence or affect a person's body image negatively or positively: the attitudes of primary caregivers, most often parents; standards determined by society of what is or is not acceptable physically; and a person's peer group. The influence of one's parents is very strong. If a parent has difficulty accepting his or her own body, it makes sense that it will be particularly hard for that parent to accept and be supportive of the changes in his or her adolescent. Along with these bodily changes are issues surrounding independence and autonomy. An adolescent begins to distance himself or herself from parents, gravitating more toward friends. The ability of a mother or father to respond positively or not to a son's or daughter's bodily and emotional changes is a large factor in that teen developing "self-shame" and "body shame."[7]

Factor two, the standards of physical acceptability set by the culture is particularly traumatic for girls. If a teen does not measure up to the cultural ideal, she may feel shame. It is nearly impossible to resolve the conflict between one's real and ideal body image. When comparing herself to that ideal, a teen girl will not measure up, particularly if she is unable to see her body realistically. The importance of a girl's appearance is stressed again and again by the mass media, even in children's books. For young girls, body image is extremely important, and they learn to form relationships often based on the acceptability of their bodies.[8]

The third influential factor is the attitude of one's peer group. Assuming a central role in an adolescent's life, peers replace family. The peer group also has standards related to authority figures, dress codes, sexual mores, social and academic performance, and appearance, among other things. All adolescents know, or assume, that there is a connection between physical attractiveness and popularity. And if their peer group is focused around an activity such as a sport that requires a certain weight or body type (such as dancing or swimming), there will be additional pressure.

There are sports that emphasize the importance of maintaining a lean body appearance and may be responsible for an increased risk of eating disorders. Champions like Cathy Rigby and Nadia Comaneci have told their stories of struggles with anorexia and bulimia. In her book *Little Girls in Pretty Boxes*, Joan Ryan writes about the making and breaking of gymnasts and figure skaters. For every girl who makes it into the spotlight of fame and fortune, there are many who do not, and, in the process, become humiliated and broken by the work and pressure. Some athletes spend countless hours intensively training for their sport while practicing dangerous eating patterns in an attempt to lower their percentage of body fat. This practice often leads to eating disorders among athletes.

Annie

Annie couldn't get "thin enough," especially if she was going to look like the models in Glamour magazine. When she was an athlete in high school, she was proud of her athletic body. Her weight stayed around 130 to 135 pounds while she was running track. Before her eating disorder began, Annie reported being very energetic, a leader with lots of friends. During the most active phase of her illness, she says, she was almost bedridden. She was constantly tired, would "fly off the handle, and perceived that all statements were aimed at her."

While practicing her eating disorder, Annie said she hated herself. "I felt unworthy and basically stopped all social activities." She avoided answering the phone and felt hopeless most of the time. She couldn't imagine a positive future and continually felt confused and paranoid.

When asked what advice she would give to young teens, Annie replied, "Every individual has a body weight normal for their body . . . accept it and keep in tip-top shape and be proud." Annie also warns "skinny is not beauty. Toned muscles and curves are. The models and actresses are not as they appear."

Most important, says Annie, is "don't lose your identity. If you feel you're lacking attention, don't get it by getting sick. You are the one who suffers the most . . . believe in yourself." The turning point for Annie was when she began to realize how worried and tired her husband had become, the anger she felt toward her parents, and the desire to lead an active life again.[9]

Cultural Message

The cultural message is clear: Slimness is essential. This message is transmitted through many sources: family, peer group, teachers, coaches, books, magazines, etc. Teens try to behave in ways that go along with the beliefs and behaviors of their friends and the groups to which they belong. There are extraordinary cultural persuasions to diet. People are led to believe that all of life's problems can be solved by dropping pounds. People are promised success and a complete transformation if only they are thin.[10]

What is confusing, though, is that at the same time, much is done to encourage people to eat a lot and gain weight. Fast-food restaurants are everywhere, bombarding people with advertisements that talk them into wanting these foods. People are constantly tempted with jingles such as "bet you can't eat just one!" At many of the activities in which people are involved, food is served: recreational events, socializing, weddings, funerals, and cookouts. There are some ethnic groups, for instance, in which eating together is a cultural event. Often, the food served is healthy. At many gatherings, however, the type and amount of food does not lend itself to healthy, balanced eating.

Going through adolescence is hard enough, and teens often feel out of step. Feelings of isolation and of being different are common, so they are constantly trying to figure out who they are. A person's self-concept, or how one thinks of oneself, develops through interacting with others. Adolescence is a time when girls are aware of other girls who seem more successful and attractive than themselves. Comparing themselves to their peers, they feel self-conscious and inadequate. So they search for the magic cure and focus on a diet as their ticket to success.

When physical changes occur during adolescence, they do not do so in a straight line. The adolescent growth spurt, body shape and weight changes, hormones, and sexual maturing largely impact the adolescent's personality and the way she behaves. Together, the attitudes and values from the culture and from the adolescent's family affect how she reacts to the changes in her body. So developing a comfortable body image is a major task for any adolescent.[11]

Learning "who am I" is critical for an adolescent and means forming a new body image and learning to match up one's concept of self with one's actual physical self. This image that is formed in adolescence is carried with a person throughout his or her life.

A Reasonable Approach

Recently, a number of newspaper and magazine articles have focused attention on the link between the pressure to be thin and eating disorders. There is also a trend toward using larger models, as well as an antidieting movement. It would seem that with these trends the idealized image would not be so important. Yet this image is still being aspired to by girls and boys alike. Hollywood icons are still scrutinized for how many pounds have been lost or gained. Why do so many continue to buy into this image, and what is so wrong with people the way they are?[12]

The inner emptiness experienced by the person with an eating disorder cannot be healed by food or by having the ideal body. What is missing can only be healed through self-acceptance, for a person to be able

Amy

Amy's highest weight was 145 pounds, her lowest 120 pounds. Her eating disorder started at one end of the anorexia/bulimia scale, when she began starving herself. After beginning to eat more and gaining twenty pounds, she then began to binge and purge. "I've always had a distorted body image," confessed Amy, "even before the disorder. Some days I think I'm thin, and some days I think I'm huge." Before her eating disorder began, Amy believed she had high self-esteem; or at least she thought she did. Who she is now, she's not quite sure.

Amy's eating disorder began after her boyfriend broke up with her. She initially lost seventeen pounds, all the time trying to be perfect. She weighed herself at least six times a day, planned out her binges, and constantly thought about food. "Stay away from society pressure," advises Amy, ". . . magazines, TV, etc.— most of these models are unhealthy anyway."

For Amy, food and weight were not the issues. She could not control her feelings, she admits, but she could control her weight. "It left me with no feelings at all, good or bad," she says. What she experienced instead was severe depression. She believed that if she was thinner, she would be happier.[13]

to accept his or her strengths as well as weaknesses. It also involves breaking away from the cultural message that slimness is essential.

Striving to wake up each morning and like what one sees in the mirror should be each person's goal—to learn to love oneself just as one is and to stop aspiring to unreal body shapes. Placing so much emphasis on a perfect body image leaves a person with less energy for developing the unique parts of himself or herself.

Dying to Be Thin

1. **When you look at many of the models in a fashion magazine, you think to yourself . . .**

   a. I'm really depressed. I'll never look like that.

   b. I think they're attractive (but you have little reaction).

   c. the models are too thin.

   d. I'm never going to look at this magazine again!

2. **You have a chance at a starring role in the school play. The only drawback is you've got to stay after school for practice four days out of five. This means you won't be able to exercise on those days. You . . .**

   a. decline the role because you'd rather limit your chances of doing anything new than gain any weight.

   b. feel really great and decide you'll bike to school whenever possible.

   c. become depressed. You never let anything interfere with your exercising everyday; sometimes two and three times a day.

3. **You're on the school gymnastics team, and your coach is strict about all gymnasts keeping in shape. This means you're expected to diet at all times to avoid gaining any weight. This makes you feel . . .**

   a. as though your worth depends only on how well you perform for the team.

   b. something is not quite right. You know you can eat healthy and still stay in shape.

   c. the coach is probably right, after all, he's the coach.

4. **When you're able to control your weight, you feel . . .**
   a. powerful and able to get attention.
   b. pleased and glad you feel good about yourself in other areas, too.
   c. you can get other girls to envy you.

5. **You're walking on the sidewalk and pass by a big picture window. You catch a glimpse of your reflection in the glass. Your first thought is . . .**
   a. I look pretty darn good in these pants and blouse.
   b. (You barely even notice yourself and keep walking.)
   c. man, I'm really a big cow!

6. **A healthy body image to you means . . .**
   a. having a body that looks like the model's in the fashion magazine.
   b. how comfortable or satisfied you feel about yourself as a person.
   c. when you're happy, you feel fine about how you look, but when you're sad, you hate the way you look.

7. **For you, being thin . . .**
   a. means I'm way cool.
   b. isn't the most important thing in the world.
   c. is more important than anything else.

8. **When developing an ideal body image, most people pay attention to parents, friends, and magazine advertisements. What's really important to remember is . . .**

   a. to take what you like and disregard what you don't like.

   b. you'd better be in style or you'll be a nobody.

   c. if you don't look like your friends who are thin, you must be inadequate.

9. **When you're dissatisfied with your body image, your total self-esteem suffers. This is when you should begin to . . .**

   a. talk your feelings over with someone you trust and figure out how you can feel better.

   b. think more about how many physical shortcomings you have.

   c. believe if you lose more weight, you'll feel better about yourself.

10. **You're a prime candidate for becoming anorexic or bulimic if you . . .**

    a. are usually realistic about your physical appearance and accept how you look.

    b. can accept compliments about your looks.

    c. buy into the "thin is cool" mentality and attempt to achieve that image at all costs.

Answers, page 125

4

The Inner Compass: Identity and Self-esteem

What is the answer to the question, "Who am I?" What is an identity? It is the knowledge of who a person is. It is made up of all the talents, strengths, and weaknesses a person has. It is what makes a person unique and separate from every other person in the world. It is part of the challenge of the teen years to define identity because, in childhood, one's identity is spelled out by one's parents and family. For example, parents may say, "He's just like his father," or "She's got a sense of humor just like Aunt Susy." But in adolescence, a person begins to explore a wider world beyond the family, and so one's identity usually needs to expand and change in response to new experiences.

Sometimes this quest for identity can be scary. Facing the unknown waters of adolescence and defining oneself as an individual, separate from family, can be frightening. It may seem safer to keep the familiar identity of childhood. Or a person may find an unhealthy behavior to cling to and claim as his or her identity. Misuse of alcohol and other drugs or gang involvement are some examples of unhealthy behaviors. Another example is the way an eating disorder can become one's identity.

A Sense of Identity

Many people with eating disorders, especially anorexia nervosa, say they did not have a sense of identity before the disorder began. Suzanne says she felt "totally passive about life. I didn't seem to be a person. I needed other people for everything."[1]

According to eating-disorder expert Hilda Bruch, many of these anorexic girls grew up satisfying their parents' needs at the expense of their own. These girls became compliant, always pleasant, and unquestioning. Although they seem very mature and responsible, they did not develop a sense of their worth as an individual person or a sense of caring about their own feelings and needs.[2]

In her book, Cherry Boone describes her relationship with her parents as "excessively close" during her teen years. Because she shared all her feelings and anxieties with her parents, her sense of herself as an individual may have gotten lost in the process.

Sheila MacLeod writes the "onset of puberty is the most important factor for a girl predisposed to anorexia nervosa . . . because then she *will* rebel." MacLeod, who also suffered from anorexia nervosa, says she knew when she was twelve that she did *not*

Natalie (cont'd)

Once I started dieting, the weight dropped off pretty fast. In six months, I'd lost so much weight, Mom sent me to a doctor. At that time I weighed 130 pounds (remember that Natalie is five feet eleven inches tall).

The doctor ordered me to stop dieting. He was concerned about the large amount of weight I'd lost. I thought, "Who are you to tell me how to run my life?!" I decided to ignore what he said, and I kept right on losing weight. This was the first time in my whole life I'd gone against what others wanted me to do and did what I wanted to do instead.

Natalie is an example of using an eating disorder as an identity. She began by deciding to continue to lose weight. Until that time, she worked very hard to please everyone so she would be liked. She did not have much of an identity of her own. She knew she was a good student, a good athlete, a good daughter, a good friend . . . but who was she on the inside? Who was the real Natalie?

Natalie's inner compass, made up of her self-identity and self-esteem, was practically nonexistent. She had very little inner guidance to help her navigate the turbulent waters of adolescence. She could not decide what college to attend, let alone what career to pursue. She relied on her parents or her friends to tell her what decisions to make. She also relied on them to make her feel worthwhile. With her best girlfriend and boyfriend gone, she felt worthless.

When the doctor ordered her to stop dieting, Natalie rebelled. She continued to diet, became anorexic, and felt that for the first time in her short life, she knew who she was: someone who was in complete control of her body/herself. She was completely thin and completely in control. Her anorexia became the center of her conscious identity. Inwardly, however, she never felt thin enough and secretly struggled to ignore her physical weakness and need for food.[3]

want to grow up. Because she was anorexic, she had no menstrual periods, her bone growth slowed, and she remained short and tiny for years. Anorexia became her identity. She did not have to try to navigate adolescence and become an adult. According to MacLeod, "Anorexia nervosa is fundamentally about an identity crisis."[4]

Katherine Byrne, the mother of a former anorexic, said the disorder gave her daughter an "unassailable identity." People might quibble whether a girl is pretty or not or has a good voice or is the best cheerleader, but no one can argue whether a girl who is five feet three inches tall and eighty pounds is thin.[5] This then becomes the identity.

Many people with eating disorders know what it means to be caught up in an identity crisis. To have a strong identity means to accept one's uniqueness and also have that uniqueness accepted by loved ones. Natalie, for example, was not accepting of her unusual height. She believed others would not accept her either. A crisis occurred when the two people who did accept her (her best girlfriend and boyfriend) were suddenly gone from her life. She was left feeling like a freak and exposed to others who she believed saw her the same way. Like other girls who find this identity crisis impossible to resolve, she turned to anorexia: Now she was thin, and others agreed with her. Conflict resolved . . . at least for the moment.

Natalie said her insides (feeling miserable) did not match her outsides (looking attractive and successful), and so people did not know or understand the real Natalie. In a sad way, once she lost more weight and began to look awful, her "outsides" came to more truly reflect her inner feelings.

Finding Oneself

compass—A device used to tell direction; used to guide a person from where he or she is to where he or she wants to be; useful on journeys of exploration in unknown places.

identity—The individual qualities that make up a person. The search for identity is one of the major developmental tasks of adolescence. It is normal for teens to explore various identities in their quest to discover who they are.

identity crisis—Being unsure of how one feels about oneself, especially regarding one's values, goals, and origins. This condition frequently occurs during adolescence due to growing up in a period of rapid change and disruptive conditions.

self-esteem—This is the value a person places on himself or herself. If a teen believes that he or she is a worthwhile person, the teen is more likely to make healthy decisions for himself or herself.

Who am I? Natalie and other people with eating disorders might answer, "I am a thin person," and appear satisfied with that answer. Yet, on the inside, people with eating disorders rarely feel either thin enough or satisfied with themselves. Being thin does not begin to describe the rich beauty of Natalie's character and personality. The search for identity takes time, but the reward is great: getting acquainted with the wonderful, unique individual one is.

Self-esteem: How Do I Measure Up?

What is high self-esteem? It is having a good opinion of oneself. It means having a realistic understanding of one's strengths as well as weaknesses and realizing that one's positive qualities outweigh the negative qualities. It means believing one is attractive and worthwhile, and is a good person. Most importantly, having high self-esteem means feeling that one is doing a good job of measuring up to personal expectations regarding behavior, appearance, and character.

However, there can be many threats to a person's self-esteem. Excessive teasing, ridicule, or criticism can lead a person to believe he or she is not worth much. The person might begin to believe he or she is bad or stupid or ugly or fat. The teen might even begin to call himself or herself those names, as if a mental tape recorder had recorded all the bad things people had said to be heard over and over again. When a person believes he or she is bad, that person may begin to make bad choices. After all, if someone is not worth much, what difference does it make what he or she does? In an attempt to stop thinking about how much he or she dislikes himself or herself, the teen may make choices that may seem exciting or attractive but actually are harmful. Using alcohol or other drugs, engaging in irresponsible sexual behavior, and other self-destructive behaviors, such as an eating disorder, are a few examples.

Low self-esteem can affect a teen's life in other ways, too. Low self-esteem saps initiative. It leaves a person feeling he or she cannot try new things, meet new people, or take healthy risks. A boy who is self-conscious about his weight might not want to participate in gym class. Or he might be uncomfortable taking a shower after class because he fears ridicule. Low self-esteem can drain the fun of being a teenager right out of his life.

Low self-esteem lies at the very heart of many teenage problems. It is a very important factor in eating disorders. Many people with eating disorders have said their self-esteem was low before the disorder began.

"When I was feeling bad and not worth much, but I was thin, and people found me attractive, it was very comforting," said Natalie, who had anorexia. Yet this comfort was not enough. Natalie learned in recovery to solve her inner problems so that she was as attractive on the inside as she was on the outside. "That is the only long-term solution," Natalie said when describing her recovery from her eating disorder. Her self-esteem grew stronger as she gained some weight during recovery and became physically and psychologically healthier. She began to feel more attractive and worthwhile. Her feelings inside finally matched her outside appearance.

Natalie found ways to increase her self-esteem through therapy. However, even if someone does not need therapy, he or she can do some things to maintain healthy self-esteem. Healthy self-esteem is based mostly on a person's inner qualities, and to some extent on one's accomplishments, but not on outward appearances or possessions.

One technique that increases self-esteem is called an "affirmation." To do this, a teen would think of a very positive statement she feels is true about herself. Then she would make a habit of repeating this statement to herself many times during the day. Some examples are "I am a good person" or "I am a hard worker" or "I am a good friend." These positive statements then work as a counterbalance to any negative statements she hears during the day and help her maintain a positive outlook and healthy self-esteem.

Finding the Way

A teen's identity and self-esteem form the inner compass that can help guide him or her through the exciting yet turbulent years of adolescence. It is a normal part of a teen's growing-up years to explore different parts of his or her personality until becoming acquainted and comfortable with who he or she really is. Unfortunately, an eating disorder prevents this normal process from happening. Identity gets stuck on the idea of being extremely thin, and self-esteem sinks to an extremely low level. The inner compass stops working.

Knowing Yourself

1. **Your English teacher assigns a speech to be given in front of the whole class in three days. You . . .**

   a. moan and groan and wish it were all over.

   b. ask your mom to get you into a different English class.

   c. tell yourself that it's not so bad, even though it makes you a little nervous, and start working on it.

2. **Your friends ask you what your best quality is. You . . .**

   a. aren't sure what to say.

   b. tell them it's that you're easy to get along with, since you have so many friends.

   c. don't think you have a best quality.

3. **You have been asked to be in charge of the school dance next month. You've never done this before. You . . .**

   a. go ballistic and refuse.

   b. ask for more time to think it over for fear you can't do it.

   c. agree to do it, because you believe you can do it.

4. **You're shopping for new clothes with your best friend. You find three really cool sweaters, and you want them all. You . . .**

   a. ask your friend to decide for you.

   b. spend a lot of time trying to decide exactly which one will be the one everyone will like.

   c. decide which one you really like best and buy it.

5. **Your phone rings all the time. Your friends seem to laugh a lot when you're around. You get invited to a lot of parties. You think it's because . . .**

   a. you're a lot of fun to be around.

   b. you don't know why these things happen.

   c. you're rich and they like all the presents you buy for them.

6. **You came home an hour late last night. Your parents were mad and yelled at you. You . . .**

   a. yelled back at them.

   b. cried and said it would never happen again.

   c. apologized.

7. **You usually get *A*'s and *B*'s on your schoolwork. Sometimes your friends say it is because you are "brownnosing" the teacher. You . . .**

   a. get embarrassed and start turning in sloppier work.

   b. know it's because you take pride in your work, and ignore the teasing.

   c. decide to get new friends.

8. **Sometimes people say you're too fat or too loud or too smart. You . . .**

   a. feel hurt, and try to avoid those people.

   b. find things to criticize about them.

   c. think you're okay just as you are.

Answers, page 125

5

Distorted Thinking, Mood Swings, and Stress

---

he September after high school graduation, I went to college," said Natalie (who has related the story of her battle with anorexia in this book). "I only lasted a couple of weeks because I had lost so much weight. I weighed only seventy pounds. I was actually too weak to carry my books or open the doors to the classroom buildings. I was humiliated by this and angry at myself because, after all, I was an athlete! But then I'd rationalize to myself, 'Well, if I ate like a pig like everyone else does, I could carry my books and open doors like everyone else, too!'"[1]

What did Natalie mean by "rationalize"? To rationalize something means to make excuses that sound good but are not really accurate. Natalie did not need to "eat like a pig" to be strong enough to carry her books or open doors. She only needed to eat in a normal, healthy way. She was excusing her weakened condition by pretending it was not really the problem; the real problem (in Natalie's mind) was that other people "ate like pigs." Since she refused to be a pig like other people, of course she couldn't open doors! Her rationalization included a sense of being better than other people, since she was not a pig like they were.

Distorted Thinking

Rationalization is an example of the distorted thinking that occurs with an eating disorder. So, too, is the sense of being better than others, called "superiority." Sheila MacLeod wrote that when she was anorexic and had lost a lot of weight and no longer had menstrual periods, she felt she "had become pure and clean and therefore, superior to those around me . . . I was virtually beyond criticism."[2]

Another example of distorted thinking is perfectionism. This means demanding of oneself and others a higher quality of performance than is actually required. Anorexia nervosa includes a lot of searching for perfection. Anorexic people want to achieve the "perfect" weight, or to find the "perfect" food. Cathy Devlin is a dietician who has worked with many anorexic people. One of her biggest challenges has been to help her clients become more flexible and less perfectionistic. "Many of my clients look for the 'perfect' food . . . the food that will sustain life but has no fat and few calories. Or they set their target weight unrealistically low," said Cathy. "One client told me, in tears, that she was getting much too fat. In reality, she'd lost six pounds!"[3]

Julie is an example of someone searching for the perfect food. "I'd play a game with myself to see how few calories I could consume," she said. "I'd see what food, with the fewest calories, would sustain me. The winner? It was a small packet of instant cream of wheat, mixed with water, not milk. It had fifty calories. That's all I'd eat until dinner."[4]

Mood Swings

Not only do anorexia nervosa and bulimia affect a person's thinking, these disorders also make a big impact on a person's moods. When bulimia begins, the person may feel elated at having found an "easy" way to lose weight. With anorexia, the person may experience euphoria, an exaggerated feeling of well-being as a result of highly restrictive eating. Marilyn Lawrence described her euphoria at her weight loss as if she had won a prize. She said, "I've won! I AM somebody now!"[5] When Sheila MacLeod weighed eighty pounds, she wrote, "I was beautiful. I was completely myself, the way I was supposed to be. As more of my skeleton emerged, I felt it was my true self emerging."[6]

She also wrote, "When I managed to convert my body into something very trim and neat . . . I became quite lively, hard-working and . . . well-organized." She found herself full of energy and high spirits and started practicing tennis for the first time in her life. She practiced so often and so intensely, she became quite a good tennis player.[7]

The euphoria and elation and excess energy do not last long, however. Soon the person plunges into equally intense negative feelings. Then the elation and euphoria may recur, so the person is on an emotional roller coaster. These highs and lows, or mood swings, are very apparent to loved ones. In fact, this may be one of the first behavioral signals that something is wrong.

"Either I was mad and 'bitchy' and wanted to be alone," Erin said of her bulimic mood swings, "or I was practically clinging to people, saying 'Please, please be my friend.' When I was actively bulimic and throwing up all the time, I acted happy, though physically I felt terrible. When I tried to stop throwing up, I was always bitchy."[8]

When Paula Abdul described her experience of bulimia, she said it got worse after she filed for divorce in May 1994. "I was so sad, I just needed to be filled up. It was like I was trying to fill a big empty hole. I couldn't stop eating."[9]

The Role Stress Plays in Eating Disorders

Growing up has never been easy. Throughout history, adolescents have had to face hard work, famine, war, and many other challenges on their journey to adulthood. In the 1990s, things have changed. Teens do not have to do backbreaking physical labor, but they must spend more years in preparation for their life's work than ever before. In addition, some challenges are new. The grim terror of AIDS makes emerging sexuality dangerous, yet teens are coaxed and encouraged by some parts of society to be sexually active at an ever earlier age. School violence has dramatically increased, and gangs are a presence in many teens' lives. All of this spells *stress* in a big way.

How do teens react to stress? Many find positive ways to use the stress to help them grow stronger and more mature. However, some turn to alcohol and other drugs to cope. And some, not aware of other options available to them, become overly involved with food, diet, or exercise for stress relief.

Lawrence wrote, "How very safe it feels to live within and behind the walls of your solution (i.e., eating disorder). . . . your anorexia protects you; although at times it is terribly painful and distressing to mind and body, it feels as though YOU are safe inside."[10]

Lillie Weiss, a psychologist who treats bulimic patients, would agree. A typical patient binged because "it calmed me down . . . right away." Eating lots of favorite binge foods brought comfort, at least temporarily.[11]

When Lisa Messenger was in recovery from bulimia, she longed for her old candy-cookie-cake binge routine. This was because she found these foods soothed her stressed-out feeling and helped her feel comfortable. Bingeing helped divert her attention from the stress she was facing and to forget the rest of life for the moment.[12]

Nell would vomit when under stress. After she threw up, all her stress and bad feelings were gone . . . for the moment. Later on, or the next day, she felt depleted and depressed.[13]

Family Stress. Many young people who succumb to eating disorders feel family pressure to achieve and/or behave extremely well. Although setting high standards for achievement and behavior can be a positive thing to do, if overdone, such demands for excelling can lead to problems.

According to Cherry Boone, "being Pat Boone's daughter was very much like being a celebrity's kid and a preacher's kid at the same time. Maintaining the Boone image was like balancing on a tightrope."[14]

Sheila MacLeod was designated the "clever" one in her family. She was the only one to go to college. She experienced great pressure to achieve.[15]

Both Cherry and Sheila were the oldest girls in their families. It is not unusual for those who have anorexia nervosa to be firstborn in their family. Many experts have noticed that large numbers of girls with anorexia are the oldest child or the oldest girl in their families.

People who succumb to an eating disorder may be reacting to stress they feel as an individual. Or it may happen that their families are also under stress. In the examples that follow, also notice the recurring theme of the loss of a loved one.

Erin said her family had problems long before her bulimia began. Her older brother was alcoholic and suicidal since age fifteen. Her mother, to whom Erin was very close, went through years of hospitalizations due to cancer. When her mother died, Erin went to live with her dad. He travelled a lot as part of his job. That is when Erin became bulimic.[16]

Sheila MacLeod was sent away to a boarding school at a young age. She did not like it there. When she was twelve, she got into trouble and was "demoted" in privileges, so the younger girls were placed ahead of her. She felt humiliated. At that same time, her best friend left the school. Sheila begged her parents to let her leave too, but they refused. She had no money to use to run away. She had no one with whom to talk.

Feeling stressed, trapped, and worthless, she became anorexic.[17]

Nancy Thode, M.S.W., compares family stress to an overflowing bucket. "Imagine a stress bucket that sits in the middle of the living-room. All the stress experienced or inherited by each family member gets poured into the bucket. A symptom in the family such as an eating disorder is an indication that the bucket has overflowed."[18]

The Reaction to Stress

High stress levels can result in very real physical changes in a person's body. This is called the "fight or flight" reaction because in prehistoric times people needed to be able to fight off a dangerous predator, like a saber-toothed tiger, or run away from it. Although saber-toothed tigers are gone, human bodies respond the same way: breathing gets fast so more oxygen gets to arms and legs; stored sugar and fats pour into the blood for quick energy; the heart speeds up and blood pressure rises to get enough blood to arms and legs; blood clotting is increased to protect against injury; muscles tense for action; digestion stops so blood can go to muscles and brain; perspiration increases; adrenalin pours into the bloodstream; and pupils dilate, allowing more light to enter the eye.

The problem in today's world is that people no longer need to flee saber-toothed tigers, or any other kind! People no longer need the fight/flight response for survival as did cavemen and cavewomen. Yet the same physiological reactions occur now as they did in the dawn of history. If a person in the 1990s has frequent fight/flight reactions throughout the day and does not find a constructive way to release the adrenalin and muscle tension, he or she can suffer physical consequences. Unrelieved stress can be related to many ailments, such as high blood pressure, headaches, arthritis, colitis, diarrhea, asthma, cardiac and circulatory problems, and muscle tension.

What Is Stress? Understanding stress is not as easy as it might seem. Everyone experiences stress, but some people get more stressed out than others. And to make it more complicated, the same event that stresses a person one day might not feel stressful on another day!

Most people think of stress as an event that happens outside of them. Taking a math test, having an argument with parents, or losing a volleyball game can all be stressful events (stressors). But taking a math test when a person studied hard and is confident of passing is very different from taking the same test when the person forgot to study—same test, but different stress level. The difference lies within the person taking the test:

Stress Formula

Well-prepared = low stress
Unprepared = high stress

So the stress formula could read:

Stressor (math test) + person (inner state: prepared or not) = stress level

Therefore, although no one can control what events happen in a person's life (for example, when math tests are scheduled, friends move away, sickness, or death), each person *can* control how he or she will respond to the stressor. For example, a student can choose to study for a math test or not. A person can find healthy, positive ways to respond to the stressful events that happen in everyone's life.

Positive Ways to Respond to Stress

There are many positive ways to respond to stress. Some ways counteract the physical part of stress, other ways soothe the emotional part of stress.

Physical Stress Relievers. The antidote for stress is relaxation. There are many ways to relax muscles (see sidebar). Learning to breathe in a relaxed way or to stretch and relax tense muscles helps rid the body of stress. The more ways a person learns to relax muscles, the better equipped he or she is to deal with stress.

Ways to Relieve the Emotional Part of Stress. The emotional part of stress is best dealt with by learning to identify feelings and then learning to express them appropriately. Weiss, when writing about her eating disorder, said she learned that many people have trouble expressing anger in a constructive way. One woman struggling with bulimia described it by saying, "I literally end up swallowing my anger and then spitting it back up."[19] Weiss also learned that many people, including those with eating disorders, are not very assertive. That means they do not speak up for themselves. As Weiss writes, "You'll find that saying 'no' and not feeling guilty about it can become a habit that will reduce stress."[20]

10 Great Relaxers

Relax your muscles:

1. Get a massage. Have a friend give you a back and neck rub. A professional massage is even better.
2. Relax your breathing. Stress can trigger shallow, rapid breathing. Slow down. Take some deep, slow breaths. Feel the air fill your lungs all the way to the bottom. Then slowly let it out.
3. Stretch the stress away. Try neck rolls to get rid of the pain in the neck caused by stress. Hang your head over, limp as a rag doll, to ease the tension in the back.
4. Soak in the tub. Try this for at least thirty minutes to feel really relaxed.
5. Exercise. Fifteen minutes of aerobic exercise such as walking, jogging, or biking is a great way to reduce stress.

Relax your feelings:

1. Write your feelings down in a Feelings Journal.
2. Find someone to whom you can talk about how stressed you feel. This could be a friend, family member, or school counselor.
3. Try laughing. Read a funny book, watch a funny movie, talk to a funny friend.
4. Or try crying. This can be an excellent way to "let it all out" and can reduce tension. Read a sad story, watch a sad movie, listen to a sad song.
5. Do something that is fun. When you are enjoying yourself, it is hard to feel stressed. When you are finished having fun, you can come back to deal with the stressor with a fresh perspective.

Many books are available and classes are taught on how to become more assertive. Another way to learn to express feelings appropriately is to write them down in a Feelings Journal. This is like a diary. However, a diary records what a person *did* during the day. A Feelings Journal records how a person *felt* during the day.

Another helpful stress reliever is to develop healthy relationships with family and friends. When stress is high, it is great to have a loved one lend a listening ear or give a hug. When relationships are not healthy, it may be helpful to talk to a school counselor or social worker about how to improve these relationships.

Relieving stress and increasing relaxation are helpful for everyone, whether or not they have an eating disorder. In fact, developing healthy stress relievers is an important part of protecting oneself from succumbing to an eating disorder. Natalie, Sheila, Erin, and all the other people in the book got into eating disorders in part because of stress. They each experienced a lot of stress in their lives, combined with the loss of loved ones. They felt they had no one with whom to talk who would really understand them. They felt lost, confused, even trapped . . . and did not know where to turn for help. Their lives felt out of control, so they tried to control their bodies through starvation or purging. This led to serious problems as explained in Chapter 6.

6

The Consequences of Anorexia and Bulimia

T he physical problems associated with eating disorders can be many. The National Association of Anorexia Nervosa and Associated Disorders (ANAD) provides a partial list of physical problems brought about by eating disorders and how these problems can cause both internal and external problems.

Physical Problems of Eating Disorders

Parts of the body that may be affected by eating incorrectly, or abusing food, especially in anorexia, include the skin, salivary glands, teeth, hair, muscle, heart, liver, kidneys, and bones. In girls, the menstrual cycle is often affected, the menstrual period stopping altogether. Someone may also have stomach pain and bloating, and her stomach might become slightly distended after eating. Swelling and puffiness, mostly around the ankles and feet, sometimes occur if someone suffers from malnutrition, vomits a lot, or uses a lot of laxatives. If the body fails to take in or retain the amount of food and fluids it needs, it can result in constipation.[1]

Other effects that may come from starvation might include being preoccupied with food or having the urge to eat unusual combinations of foods. Some people worried about their weight often drink large amounts of coffee, tea, or spice mixtures, and some chew gum because they believe it will cause them to be less hungry. If they do not eat, they reason, they will lose weight faster.

Changes in a person's emotions also take place as a result of unhealthy eating. Some of these new feelings include depression, anxiety, and irritability as well as problems concentrating or remembering things. Restricting ourself from eating slows down the body's metabolism. Practicing such eating habits as skipping breakfast and lunch, but eating a normal portion or large portion dinner can actually cause weight gain.

Improper eating habits can also lead to bingeing, or eating large amounts of food quickly. Without the proper balance in food groups, a person experiences strong cravings, which can lead to eating the wrong foods, especially "junk" foods.

For those who eat compulsively, the physical consequences often consist of weight gain, sometimes obesity (or weight that exceeds 20 percent of a person's normal body weight); an increased risk of high blood pressure; heart attacks and strokes; and problems with bones and joints. These physical problems are, of course, possibilities that may occur over a long period of time. What it shows, though, is that it is very important for the human body to have the proper nutrition.

Why Do People Eat and Exercise in Unhealthy Ways?

Although there is more than one theory about why people develop an eating disorder, behaviors are often used to cope with stress, painful feelings, and/or other troubles. Teens who have not learned healthy, effective ways of dealing with their feelings cope by overeating, undereating, or a combination of the two. A person who develops an eating disorder probably did not learn how to handle the everyday frustrations and intense emotions that everyone faces from time to time.

When asked what they get out of their eating disorder (what benefits), people answer that they feel in control when they are eating or that they feel special and important when they lose weight. Following a routine and a ritual gives them a feeling of perfect control, or the illusion of being in control. This ultimately backfires, and the person ends up feeling out of control.

For some, eating is a very emotional experience. They eat when they are lonely, bored, frustrated, or feeling empty. Food makes them feel loved. Eating may feel safer for some than reaching out to other people for comfort. It is not uncommon to hear someone say that her eating disorder gives her an identity, it defines who she is. She is not always sure who she is apart from how much she weighs, or what she does or does not eat.

For some people, exercise becomes an addiction, much like eating. Although it is not easy to define where healthy exercise ends and unhealthy addiction takes over, some people get so hooked they keep running or pumping iron long past where it hurts. Alberto Salazar, a star athlete who ran marathons in the 1980s, used to run 120 miles a week when he was in college. According to *Sports Illustrated* magazine, one week he suffered a foot injury (or stress fracture) and still ran 105 miles. Once he ran so hard he suffered severe heat prostration, his body temperature rising to 108 degrees![2]

For the person addicted to exercise, it is not how far one runs, rather, how one does it. The person begins to put everything into the exercising, whether it be running or any other form of exercise. The exercise begins to define who the person is. When the routine starts to run a person's life, trouble begins. The addict in his or her obsession loses perspective on how fat or fit he or she is. The person talks about it all the time and may develop an eating disorder (bulimia or anorexia) in order to keep trim.[3]

How can a person tell if he or she, or a friend, may have a problem with compulsive exercising? The person can ask himself or herself these questions: Do you exercise several hours a day and several days a week? Do you define self-worth in terms of performance? Are you fanatical about weight and diet? Do you steal time from school work or family and friends to exercise?

Nell's Turning Point. Nell, whom we met in Chapter 2, had bulimia so severely she vomited as many as twenty times a day. The physical consequences of Nell's eating disorder were many. She would cough up blood easily, get stomach cramps almost daily, experience dizziness and fainting, and her throat became very sore. She also experienced chest pains, caused by a low potassium level, and became depressed before and after purging.

The real turning point for Nell came at the end of the summer of 1992 when she was continually bingeing and purging and exercising two to three hours at a time. Bulimic since the age of twelve, Nell was obsessed with fat and weight; it peppered all her conversations with friends. One morning she just laid her head on the toilet seat and cried. It was the third time that day that she hung her head over the toilet to vomit, and it was not yet 9:00 A.M.!

With the support of her husband, Nell sought help in a hospital-based eating disorder program. Though she fought it at first, Nell gradually began to feel safe there. There were moments when she thought she could not do it. But as she began to get better, she would experience what she described as spiritual moments more often, leaving her with new feelings of peace and relief. When she was practicing her eating disorder, though, Nell did not have moments of peace. Nor did she seem to have any faith or beliefs to comfort her.

Getting better for Nell meant giving up her rituals, which included purging up to twenty times a day and weighing herself forty times a day. Her doctor suggested she get rid of the scale. After breaking it, she frantically tried to put it back together again. Finally, she committed to working with a counselor weekly at first, then monthly. She began to learn what her triggers were, those things that would set her off, such as weighing herself. One of the hardest things for Nell to change was her body image, because she believed she could never be thin enough.

Nell's advice to anyone who suspects she may have a problem with food is to get help. "Look inside yourself," says Nell. "Don't measure your worth by pounds and inches. And write down your successes, not your failures." She also reminds those who may have a problem with food that answers do not come from a scale, "only from inside yourself. No matter what size your pants are, you and your feelings are the same."[4]

How to Find Help for an Eating Disorder

If a person thinks he, or a friend, may have an eating disorder, there is more than one place he can go for help. Most schools have a social worker or counselor on staff or a school nurse. Often, these professionals know of providers in the area who specialize in eating disorders. If someone is in a crisis and needs help immediately, he can go to the nearest hospital emergency room or call a crisis hotline. The hotlines can be located in the telephone book under Crisis Intervention Services in the Yellow Pages. The hotlines are staffed by experienced and knowledgeable professionals who can talk with someone who may be in crisis or who just has questions about eating disorders.

At first, many people with eating disorders do not want treatment. How much they resist depends, in part, on how far the eating disorder has progressed. It also depends on how parents handle the situation. Sometimes parents do not, or choose not to, recognize that there may be a problem with their teenager. What is important for those who are thinking about getting help to know is that the focus of therapy is not on weight. Rather, the goal is to stop the emotional suffering that accompanies an eating disorder and to teach people how to live a normal life and to develop a healthy food plan.

In nonemergency situations, a person can also call the family doctor for an evaluation or a referral to a specialist. Most important is to ask a trusted person. Sometimes it is easier to talk to a neighbor or a family friend than it is to a parent. Sharing concerns with someone who is older is often a positive first step.

Low-cost resources that provide a sliding fee scale based on what a person can pay are usually the local community service agencies, also listed in the Yellow Pages. They can be located under Counselors, Social Services, or Family Service Agencies. Although a community agency may not have an eating-disorder specialist on staff, they can direct a person to a specialist in the community.

One of the biggest obstacles to seeking help is fear. A teen with an eating disorder may be terrified of getting fat. She may be afraid that if she gets treatment she may gain weight. In the past, some professionals even told people with eating disorders that they would "fatten them up" as part of the treatment program.

A quality treatment program will not try to "fatten up" anyone with an eating disorder. The goal is to improve a person's relationship with food. In this healing process, anorexics will restore their body to a healthy weight but will not get fat. A teen with concerns about eating disorders should not let fear of fat interfere with getting the information or help she needs.

How Can I Help a Friend Who Has a Problem with Food?

If you believe a friend or family member may have a weight disorder, you may be able to help by doing the following:

1. Talk about your concerns with a professional—school counselor, teacher, nurse—and learn about eating disorders and available resources.

2. Talk to your friend. Keep the discussion informal and private, and relate your concerns about your friend's health, not weight or appearance.

3. Tell your friend how the problem is affecting your relationship. If your friend seems to acknowledge the problem, suggest some resources.

4. Realize you may be rejected. People with a weight disorder often deny their problem because they are afraid to admit it. Don't take the rejection personally. Just try to end the conversation in a way that will make it easy for your friend to come back to the subject another time.

5. Know your limits. If you feel yourself getting mad or impatient, back off. Remember, people have to be ready.

If you are a friend of someone under eighteen with an eating disorder, tell a trusted adult—parent, teacher, coach. You are not betraying your friend's trust; you may be saving his or her life. If you think someone you know has a problem and is over eighteen years of age, encourage him or her to seek professional help. But expect your friend to resist and deny that there is anything to be concerned about. People have to be ready to get help. But when they are ready, they will remember who they can trust.

What Is an Eating Disorder?

Eating disorders are both psychologically and physiologically complex but can be characterized by an obsession about and feelings of being out of control over food, eating habits, and body image. People with eating disorders believe that thinner is better. They believe it so much that their weight and successful dieting become the measure of their self-esteem. Thinking that eating and dieting are both the cause and result of their problems, they become trapped in a vicious cycle of repeated, ritualistic, and rigid behavior focused on food. Bulimics, or those people who binge/purge, feel controlled by the circular situation that develops: anxiety leads to gorging, to fear of fat, to vomiting, to release from fear, to guilt, to anxiety, etc.

Survey data reveal that at least one member of 45 percent of U.S. households is on a diet during the course of a year. Americans spend $10 billion each year on diets and diet aids.

Anorexia nervosa, one of the eating disorders, is characterized by an obsession with thinness that results in voluntary self-starvation. Both adolescent females and males are affected. By controlling their own bodies— refusing to eat or exercising excessively—the anorexic gains a false sense of power. Some of the warning signs of anorexia are loss of 25 percent or more of one's body weight, distorted self-image (believing one is fat), an obsession with food but refusing to eat, and perfectionism.

Bulimia, also called binge-purge syndrome, is the alternating between bingeing on large quantities of food, then purging by vomiting, diuretics, and/or the use of laxatives. Bulimia usually affects women in their twenties and thirties, but men also suffer from the disorder. Warning signs of bulimia include swollen salivary glands, excusing oneself after meals to purge, dental problems from chronic vomiting, stockpiling of food, and obsession with food.

Binge-eating disorder is the eating of large quantities of food in a short period of time (like bulimia) WITHOUT purging (unlike bulimia). Like other eating disorders, strong feelings of low self-worth, guilt, shame and powerlessness are involved. Food is used to soothe or distract the binge eater from painful events or feelings.

Binge eaters are usually overweight and may become obese. Some of the medical problems from compulsively overeating include high blood pressure, diabetes, osteoarthritis, and heart problems.

There are different ideas about what causes an eating disorder. Researchers have studied the personalities, family backgrounds, genetics, environments, and biochemistry of anorexics and bulimics. The study of biological factors indicates that eating disorders run in families. And some theorists believe that anorexic girls and young women are usually shy, serious, neat, quiet, and have conscientious personalities. On the other hand, researchers believe that bulimics are more outgoing, impulsive, and emotional.

Some of the psychological symptoms of eating disorders are depression, obsessive-compulsiveness, and social withdrawal. These disturbances are caused by a person's distorted view of herself and the world around her. Another symptom is distortion of body image. Anorexics are unable to give an accurate estimate of their body weight and perceive themselves as much larger than they really are. Most feel their emaciated state is just right or too fat. In some females, menstruation has ceased.

It is also important to remember what not to do. Don't nag, beg, bribe, or plead with someone to get help. If you criticize or shame your friend, he or she will withdraw. First and foremost, respect the person's need for privacy, and only give advice when asked. Don't overestimate what you can accomplish. You can provide support and encourage your friend, but you cannot make him or her want to get help or to change.

Realize that recovery is your friend's responsibility, not yours. If your friend refuses to help himself or herself, remember only that person—not you—can cause a recovery to happen. Demonstrate how healthy people use professionals to help with their fears and anxieties.

Erin's Turning Point. For Erin, who suffered from bulimia, losing weight by vomiting up her meals was her way of staying thin. What she did not realize, though, is that vomiting does not always work in this way. In fact, much of the food that is eaten during a binge is retained by the body. And some people even gain weight.

However, people noticed and complimented Erin about how she looked, only reinforcing the delusion that vomiting worked. Every so often she would become afraid of what her father would think if he caught her practicing her eating disorder, so she would stop vomiting. Inevitably, she would gain weight. So the cycle would begin again. At her worst, Erin could not keep any food down. Her stomach would cramp and bloat, and she would be in pain.[5]

The turning point for Erin was the winter during her senior year in high school when she hit bottom. This year was hard for Erin. She would leave school at noon, go home, eat lunch, and then vomit. She was vomiting as many as two and three times a day. She had no energy and did not care about anything. She became very depressed and gave up sports and extra activities. Finally, her dad confronted her. By this time, Erin was so scared and tired, she was honest with her father and finally admitted she had a problem. When her dad asked if she wanted help, Erin said she did. After seeking help and beginning to take antidepressant medication, Erin's moods leveled off, helping her remain calm. She slowly began to accept help for herself—not for anyone else—so she could be happy.

As sometimes happens when a person takes steps to get better, Erin's good friend became angry with her. Friends of someone with an eating disorder may become threatened, scared, or jealous when the person begins to change. Perhaps they too have a problem and watching a friend get better scares them. Erin's friend's self-esteem may not have been very strong, therefore, she was not able to feel good about Erin doing something for herself.

Instead of freaking out and becoming scared and hyper the way Erin had in the past, she was able to remain calm. She decided she and her friend could work it out. Recovery for Erin has meant an improvement in her self-esteem. She admits to feeling happier and more confident about facing life's problems. Her advice to other girls who may have an eating disorder is to "be honest with yourself. Ask yourself what it is you want, not what others want for you. . . . Also," Erin advises, "don't be afraid to ask for help if you need it. It's never too late. Talk to someone you can trust—a neighbor, cousin, or anyone who's older than you."

Levels and Types of Treatment

There are a variety of possible types of treatment for eating disorders, and they vary depending upon which level of care is recommended to fit a person's need. Probably not all people with eating disorders will have a similar response to the same treatment.

Some problems take longer than others to solve. Eating disorders are usually interwoven with other struggles in a person's life, making it scary to look at and work on. There are no simple or easy answers to solving the difficulties of an eating disorder. Working on oneself and getting healthy is probably the hardest work a person with an eating disorder will face.

The first step is the most difficult. How does someone begin to ask for help? It requires taking a close look at oneself to examine flaws and difficulties. A person has to admit to himself that he can no longer take care of everything on his own. Acknowledging the need for help is 50 percent of the battle toward getting better.[6] Having an eating disorder is confusing not only for the individual, but for family and friends as well.

Evaluation. Perhaps the best place to start is with a physical and psychological evaluation. This can be done by a medical doctor, with the help of a mental health professional who specializes in eating disorders. Treatment often consists of one or more of the following: group therapy, individual and family therapy, hospitalization, nutritional counseling, medication, and/or support groups. Individual therapy with a professional trained in the area of eating disorders is the most common approach today.

Hospitalization. Although hospitalization for an eating disorder does occur, it happens infrequently. Unless there are serious medical problems, such as diabetes, or physical damage, such as stomach problems due to prolonged vomiting, a person can usually be treated on an outpatient basis. If after months of individual or group counseling a person does not improve, he may need to go into a hospital program. Supervision by doctors and/or nurses may be necessary.

Therapy. The goal of individual therapy for someone with anorexia is to help them develop a valid self-concept and to learn to do the things they perceive are right for them. A therapist works with the anorexic person to uncover his or her own abilities and resources for thinking, judging, and feeling. By becoming aware of these impulses, feelings, and needs, a person can learn to be more of an independent person.

If someone with an eating disorder requires a group setting, there are partial hospital treatment programs and more intensive outpatient programs that are provided by centers specializing in eating disorders. These programs generally meet three or four nights a week for group, individual, and family therapy. Patients are educated about eating disorders, as well as involved in a program on nutrition. The patient lives at home and continues in his or her everyday activities, such as school or outside activities. These programs work best for the person who needs a little more structure and support.[7]

If a person does not have any life-threatening medical problems, intensive outpatient therapy works well. Usually, this type of program lasts for six weeks, involves family members, and is time-consuming.

Confronting Eating Disorders

The consequences of anorexia and bulimia can be many, from physical problems to relationship problems to conflicts within oneself. There may be more than one reason why someone develops an eating disorder, but for most, it coexists with other problems in life and is used as a way of coping.

Looking at eating disorders as learned psychological patterns a person uses to help him or her deal with life is one way to understand them. Sometimes an eating disorder occurs along with such things as anxiety or pain, and the eating disorder is used as a way to cope. The eating disorder as a method for coping is one way for a person to boost low self-esteem. Through therapy, a person can learn to confront these defenses and learn new and healthier ways of coping.

It is important to remember that therapy cannot provide an immediate cure. Instead, it must be viewed as a process in which growth and change are desirable. It takes time for the self to grow, and it is this personal growth that will help the person with an eating disorder recover. The patient-therapist relationship is an important one, but the person with the eating disorder also must come to appreciate his or her own views and strengths.[8]

Making the decision to seek treatment is a major one. However, the rewards are many. For those with eating disorders, the benefits include improved physical health, better relationships, and increased self-esteem. Attempting to recover from eating disorders involves struggle and courage, but most find they can do more than they ever thought they could.

Controlled by Food

1. **You've noticed you've lost some weight recently; you think constantly about food, and you're always counting calories. You've wondered if you might have a problem with food but try not to think about it. You decide to . . .**

   a. talk to the school counselor to see if maybe you might have a problem.

   b. pretty much put it out of your mind and continue with what you're doing.

   c. look into other diets to figure out if you can lose even more weight.

2. **Your best friend suggests you try out the new buffet restaurant in town. Although you already planned on eating a light dinner at home, you say yes and join her for the buffet. You eat more than you should and feel stuffed. Afterward you feel . . .**

   a. okay about yourself—pleased you tried a new restaurant but know you probably should have eaten less.

   b. upset with yourself and decide you won't eat for two days.

   c. totally disgusted with yourself and are depressed.

3. **Unhealthy eating habits mean . . .**

   a. eating only when you're hungry.

   b. making sure you eat in a balanced way and include all the food groups.

   c. undereating, overeating, or a combination of the two.

4. **A friend of yours has lost a fair amount of weight in the last six months, hasn't had her period in over eight months, and seems to be losing the enamel off her front teeth. You think it may be because . . .**

   a. her family has poor genes.

   b. she may be suffering from an eating disorder and should probably get some help.

   c. she's just getting older and her body's changing.

5. **You notice you're eating whenever things don't go right or you've had an argument with your boyfriend. If you control what you eat, you feel special and important and usually get more attention. This reaction probably means . . .**

   a. you may have an eating disorder and use food to cope with your problems.

   b. nothing. You aren't alarmed at your behavior so you decide to ignore it.

   c. very little. After all, that's how your mom handles stress.

6. **You've been fasting for three days, drinking only a few glasses of water. You begin to feel a little depressed, anxious, and irritable. You . . .**

   a. ignore it, and remind yourself how great you'll look when you've lost all that weight.

   b. chalk it up to getting only a *B* on that last English essay.

   c. become a little concerned and decide you probably should begin to slowly eat food again.

7. **You decided recently to start taking better care of yourself. For you, this means eating more balanced meals, exercising once daily, and getting your rest. Your best friend doesn't agree that this is what you need and argues with you. You . . .**

   a. figure she's probably right and you start to diet again.

   b. freak out, become hyper, and worry constantly that she won't be your friend anymore.

   c. remain calm and tell yourself you and she can probably work it out.

8. **You've noticed your boyfriend exercises several hours a day, is a fanatic about his weight, and seems to be spending all of his free time working out instead of being with you, his friends, or his family. It's possible he may . . .**

   a. be addicted to exercising and watching his weight, so much so that it defines who he is.

   b. be practicing for the Olympics.

   c. have nothing better to do.

9. **You often have weight changes of ten or more pounds, eat when you're not hungry, and often feel depressed for no clear reason. You might . . .**

   a. be in love.

   b. just be overreacting.

   c have an eating disorder.

10. **After you break up with someone, you . . .**

   a. talk with someone about your feelings and try to resolve what's bugging you.

   b. eat everything in sight.

   c. exercise three times a day, everyday, trying to forget about him.

Answers, page 125

7

Healthy Attitudes and Practices of Weight Control

Allison and Kari, both of whom we learned were overweight in Chapter 1, took part in Physical Management classes.

"At first I was quiet and shy," said Allison. "I couldn't talk to anyone. But by the end of the program, I had really come out of my shell. I wasn't afraid to talk anymore. I learned that if I have a good opinion of myself, others will, too."[1]

Besides the development in her personality, Allison learned positive habits to last a lifetime: good nutrition, the best type of exercise for her, and working at building self-esteem. Rather than losing fifty pounds, she would lose five now, and then five more, and so on. She figured out what overall plan worked best for her and began setting goals. In a two-year period of time, Allison, in addition to losing weight, began to develop more secure self-esteem. Her advice became: "Don't be afraid to try a plan to gain fitness."

For Kari, a long history of weight gain taught her that she was not really committed to her program. Although she wanted to learn about food, nutrition, and exercise, she felt slower at it than everyone else. During her sophomore year, Kari lost forty pounds, only to gain it all back. She found out she was trying to change too fast. After a while, Kari finally understood that unless she was ready to follow a long-term program, it would not work. Kari eventually learned that she, too, had to discover what exercises were good for her and that it was important for her to motivate herself to get out and do something positive for herself. She also learned what were the best foods to eat. A food plan, made up of healthy eating habits, exercise, and behavior strategies to manage stress are all a part of what helped Kari. Adopting a plan for herself was a commitment she had to be ready to make. "Don't do it for others, do it for yourself" is Kari's advice.[2]

Successful Weight Loss: Diets Don't Work

Successful weight loss or weight control is possible once one learns the tools for normal eating. Chronic dieting does not work and, in fact, usually causes a person to gain weight. So, rather than dieting, it is better to make changes in food selections, develop an exercise plan, and work on an attitude adjustment.

Statistics tell us that only 5 percent of all dieters maintain their weight loss after one year. Considering that the average American diets three to four times a year, those statistics are not very encouraging.

Although Americans spent $10 billion in 1989 on diet aids, the bottom line is diets do not work.

Why don't diets work? Mostly because dieting often can lower the body's metabolism (the chemical changes in living cells by which energy is provided for vital processes and activities) enough to decrease the need for calories. This is done in two ways: First, a diet of less than 1,000 calories a day can cause a starvation-like state and force the body to conserve calories. In order to survive, the body will cut back its caloric needs. Therefore, a person does not lose more in the long run on a 500-calories-a-day diet than when on a 1,000-calories-a-day diet. The starvation state the body goes into can lower the metabolism for as long as one year.

Second, crash dieting can change the body's composition. For instance, if someone loses ten pounds in two weeks, most of that weight is water, some is fat, and the rest muscle. When the weight is regained, it comes back in the form of fat and water. Every diet after that can cycle this downward trend of muscle loss until the chronic dieter's percentage of body fat is changed over time, from 25 percent to 35 or 40 percent.

The scale may not show large amounts of weight change. Muscle burns more calories than fat and constant dieting may have caused a loss of large percents of what helps keep a person trim. This yo-yo effect of depriving the body and regaining weight can be harmful. It is better to not have dieted at all than to keep losing and gaining weight over and over.

A good balanced diet is essential for everyone. Rather than dreaming unrealistically about a perfect body, we each need to accept the basic physical build we have and begin, rather, to give ourselves a healthy body. Eating properly means to sit down when eating and to avoid eating on the run, if possible. Making sure to eat breakfast, lunch, and dinner each day is also helpful. Eating slowly and drinking plenty of water is important for a healthy body.

Many people grew up with old-fashioned eating habits, including such things as meat and bread and butter with every meal and always putting gravy on their mashed potatoes. Many people are unaware of what they put into their mouths. The key to developing sound eating habits is becoming aware of what is eaten and learning to make the choices that are best for one's body.

As we learned earlier, cultural and ethnic differences exist concerning food. There are basic foods, however, that make up a balanced and healthy diet, including a diet rich in carbohydrates, fruits, vegetables, fiber, low-fat dairy products, and protein. Eating in moderation is also important, particularly with red meats, polyunsaturated fats, and foods high in cholesterol. Balancing healthy foods, managing portions, and getting the proper nutrients is what leads to successful weight loss.

When trying to lose some weight, it is best to follow the recommendations of a medical doctor. Diet changes should be slow. It is not about avoiding any one type of food altogether. Rather, it involves the freedom to eat different kinds of foods in a balanced way. Without a healthy balance, a person will feel deprived, and will be more likely to overeat. By following a healthy food plan, it is possible to become comfortable with eating when hungry and letting the body dictate when it has had enough.

At times, maintaining a healthy weight becomes mundane and boring. Therefore, trying a new approach may help, such as varying meal times. Rather than eating at the same time each day, it may help to try having breakfast twenty minutes later than usual. This technique may work for some, but it is not for everyone. There are those who need more consistency, structure, and regularity.

A good basic rule is to eat only when hungry. It takes time for a person with an eating disorder to recognize the feeling of hunger. This is why it is important to begin with a food plan, planning out what to eat and recording each meal. When a person restricts herself from eating or binges, she loses touch with what hunger feels like and how to tell the difference between it and other feelings.

At times a person may notice herself reaching for food when she is not really hungry. When this happens, it is helpful to stop and think about what she is really feeling. Is it loneliness, anger, depression, or even happiness? In other words, is it really hunger that she is feeling? Choosing a different activity, such as riding a bike, walking, running, or playing soccer, teaches us to make different choices. Only when a person learns to tell the difference between hunger and other needs can she find ways to satisfy those needs.[3] Experimenting with different approaches is helpful, but knowing oneself is what works best.

Learning to Eat Right

Don't Forget the Water. Drinking plenty of water is very important. Water suppresses the appetite naturally and helps the body metabolize stored fat. A decrease in water intake will cause fat deposits to increase because the kidneys cannot function properly without enough water. One of the liver's primary functions is to metabolize stored fat into usable energy for the body. But if the liver has to do some of the kidney's work, it cannot operate to its full capacity. As a result, it metabolizes less fat, more fat remains stored in the body, and weight loss stops.

Drinking enough water is the best treatment for retaining too many fluids and feeling bloated. When the body gets less water, it perceives it as a threat to survival and begins to hold onto it. The best way to overcome water retention is to give the body plenty of water. The more overweight a person is, the more water she needs because of a larger metabolic load.

Water also helps maintain muscle tone by giving muscles their natural ability to contract and by preventing dehydration. It also helps prevent sagging skin. Water helps the body rid itself of waste by shedding metabolized fat.

On the average, eight 8-ounce glasses of water a day is adequate. That is about two quarts. If someone is overweight by twenty-five pounds or is exercising briskly or the weather is hot and dry, the amount of water should be increased. Cold water is absorbed into the system more quickly than warm water.

A Healthy Diet. A healthy diet means eating balanced meals with foods from all the food groups. These include a sufficient amount of simple and complex carbohydrates such as grains, vegetables, fruits, legumes, pasta, rice, and cereals. Generally, eating a balanced meal every four to five hours throughout the day and taking nutritious snacks, such as carrot sticks, granola bars, and fruit, to supplement meals works best for most people.[4]

If fewer than 1,000 calories a day are consumed, it is difficult for the body to get the nutrients it needs. The proper amount of calories depends on a person's age, weight, and height. Although 1,200 calories a day works well for some people, it is not the right amount for everyone. Adolescents may need more calories than adults for several reasons: Their bodies are still growing, and they are generally more active, thus, burning more calories. What is important is making sure to include a variety of foods and consuming some protein, vegetables, fruit, starches, and fat every day. Most food plans recommend six servings of breads, pastas, and rice, followed by three to four servings of vegetables, and two to three servings of fruit.[5]

An example of a 1,400-calorie-a-day diet would include about six ounces of meat (or a substitution such as cooked dry beans, nuts, or eggs) and two to three servings of milk (substituted with cheese, yogurt, tofu, or cottage cheese). Teenagers and children need more servings of milk than adults. The same 1,400-calorie diet would include four servings of vegetables, four fruits, five starches, and three fats. Serving sizes are important, as the proper portions go hand in hand with eating the right amount of nutritious foods.[6]

The main point to emphasize is that all food groups should be included in a healthy daily diet. Many people with eating disorders are afraid of eating too many carbohydrates because it has been a binge food for them or a craving they have felt the need to indulge to excess. They have to learn to slowly increase their intake of starches by eating pasta, rice, bread, and legumes. Support and reinforcement by others is important for them during this time so they learn to eat those things that are nutritious and good for their bodies.[7]

If it is recommended that someone lose some weight, it is smarter to cut down on portion size than to eliminate certain foods altogether. Each food group is essential for the body to grow and thrive. Vegetables, for instance, provide the right amount of essential vitamins, minerals, and electrolytes. By restricting food intake for a long period of time, a person will deplete his body of the vitamins and minerals needed for the body to maintain itself.

A healthy food plan includes learning to make substitutions. The fact that potato chips, candy bars, and ice cream are high in fat and low in nutrition is well known. By learning to substitute low-fat foods, such as fat-free yogurt, fruit, plain popcorn, or toast with jam, a person will be giving his body what it needs to feel full and be satisfied.

Tips to Help You Stick to a Food Plan. There are some basic rules for losing and maintaining weight that researchers seem to agree on, and that everyone can apply.

For someone who is overweight, making commitments about weight must be done in small doses. For instance, making a small commitment each day, rather than for weeks or months at a time, helps put the task in perspective. It is easier to be successful if it is known that each commitment only lasts for one day. No one can expect all of a sudden to exercise daily, for instance, if he or she has not exercised for ten years, or ever. Succeeding at small goals is manageable and more encouraging.

Attitude. Developing a positive attitude is essential to successfully controlling weight. Preoccupation with

"Losing" Tips

- ☐ Don't let anyone "love" you with food
- ☐ Eat your favorite foods in preplanned moderate fashion
- ☐ Eat to live, don't live to eat
- ☐ Drink eight 8-ounce glasses of water a day
- ☐ Set realistic goals within a limited time frame
- ☐ Remember: Success comes when looking *beyond* food

food can be distracting and makes it harder to achieve normal eating habits. Learning to eat healthily helps a person develop a positive attitude and, in turn, decreases one's preoccupation with food. Getting involved in activities that are enjoyable helps, too. It is important for a person to begin to focus on what is special about her and to use self-talk to remind herself that she is a worthwhile person.

Learning to challenge all-or-nothing thinking is essential. People with eating disorders, often perfectionists, believe that one mistake will be the end of the weight plan. Overeating or eating a piece of chocolate cake one day is not going to make someone fat. What may is an accompanying attitude of "I've really blown it now, so who cares." Simply begin again tomorrow.

When making a decision to stop dieting, many have rediscovered their sense of taste and smell, and what it is like to feel hunger and to taste foods. Becoming aware of their hunger and beginning to feel safer about responding to their appetite was a slow process but one that helped them be able to eat normally. They also began to develop a genuine sense of self-control and self-worth in the process.

If a person visualizes herself attaining her goals and imagining how she wants to look, her thoughts will be positive. Many athletes and performers use the master skill of mentally rehearsing. This can also be applied to eating by learning to develop a picture of calmly handling any eating-related trouble spots. Getting nervous and stressed out triggers nervous eating in some people. So learning alternative ways to manage stress is helpful. Practicing assertiveness and time-management skills can also help when trying to develop substitute behavior.

Exercise

In addition to food consumption, the other important part of successful weight control is exercise. Determining which type of exercise is right is the first step. Most experts agree that exercise at least three times a week for one-half hour or more is adequate to maintain health. Exercising helps the body burn more calories by raising the metabolic rate. It also helps reduce depression and generally helps a person feel better about himself or herself.

According to the President's Council on Physical Fitness and Sports, nearly half of American teenagers between twelve and twenty-one are no longer vigorously active, including a dropoff of daily enrollment in physical education classes from 42 percent in 1991 to 25 percent in 1995."[8] Only the state of Illinois requires daily physical education for every child.[9]

Why exercise? someone may ask. According to a survey in *American Averages*, some of the more obvious reasons that make sense to teens include being able to better maintain weight loss, improving balance and coordination, and gaining more control over one's life. Self-esteem is also increased, and a sense of pride and accomplishment are common by-products of keeping active. Exercise helps maintain and improve flexibility, offering such benefits as increased concentration and energy in sports and outdoor activities.[10]

The more vigorous the exercise, the more calories a person burns. An added benefit is that the body will continue to burn more calories than normal fifteen hours after a person is through exercising. Activities such as running, fast walking, bicycling, swimming, aerobic dancing, rowing, cross-country skiing, and uphill hiking are all good choices. Even such activities as walking the dog or cleaning the house burn calories. Moderate activity, such as using the stairs instead of the elevator, can improve health, speed up metabolism, and build muscle tissue.

Walking is an especially good form of exercising. Walking is aerobic (air-o-bic), which means the body is using oxygen. The idea of aerobics is to work hard enough that the heart beats faster and a person has to breathe harder. As with changing eating habits, so too with exercising: One should start out gradually. Walk for ten minutes, then twenty minutes, and so on. As a person gets into better and better shape, he or she will gradually cover more distance, and in less time.[11]

Playing basketball and/or rollerblading is great exercise; just about anything that is an aerobic type of activity promotes good health. Becoming involved in sporting activities also increases one's socialization skills. Interacting with others in team sports helps curb the tendency to become isolated. Of course, getting enough rest is also important.[12]

When performing any form of aerobic exercise, warm-ups (stretching) and cool-downs (relaxing) for five to ten minutes before beginning and again after finishing are very important. These times allow the heart rate and a person's breathing to increase and decrease slowly, without a sudden stop and start. If after exercising a person stops suddenly, he could experience dizziness, extra heartbeats, nausea, or even fainting. This happens because the blood is trapped in the suddenly unmoving muscles. The cool-down phase gives the blood a chance to return to its normal circulation levels, and the heart to its average level.

An Ideal Weight

What becomes clear when looking at teens and eating disorders is that society and the media play a large part in dictating attitudes. Young people today are increasingly bombarded by countless "perfect" body images on TV, in the movies, and throughout magazines. The 1996 Council on Size and Weight Discrimination, Inc., found that 50 percent of nine-year-old girls and 80 percent of ten-year-old girls have dieted and that anorexia has the highest mortality rate (up to 20 percent) of any psychiatric disorder.[13] For many of these girls, feeling worse about the bodies they have is the result of the stigma of being fat. Comparing themselves to these unrealistic standards can only lead to the conclusion that they are losers.[14]

Learning to develop a healthy attitude is essential to weight control, self-esteem, and committing to a healthy lifestyle. It is all right to aim for an ideal, but be sure it is a realistic one.

Are You Fit?

1. You've tried all the recent fad diets, from low or no protein to just soup and fruit. You've always managed to lose weight, but it doesn't seem to stay off. You may . . .

   a. only be getting one type of food and leaving out others, especially nutrients.

   b. be increasing your metabolism.

   c. not be trying hard enough.

2. You're exercising five days a week for half an hour each day. You don't seem to be losing weight as fast as you'd like, but you probably . . .

   a. are toning muscle and strengthening your body.

   b. should increase your exercise time to lose weight faster.

   c. should just give it up altogether.

3. You've just had a fight with your parents; you're upset and head right for the refrigerator. You polish off one carton of ice cream, a bag of oatmeal cookies, and two slices of pizza. You should . . .

   a. throw it all up immediately.

   b. try to figure out what else you can do to comfort yourself and resolve family problems.

   c. continue bingeing.

4. **Successful weight loss to you means . . .**
   a. losing five pounds a week, whether you need to or not.
   b. learning how to eat normally.
   c. trying every diet that comes along.

5. **When wanting to lose some weight, the best solution is to . . .**
   a. follow your doctor's recommendation and change your diet slowly.
   b. just not eat anything for a few days.
   c. avoid certain foods altogether.

6. **You'd like to stick to a healthy food plan. What are some good ideas to help you accomplish this?**
   a. Eat all foods one week, and fast the following week.
   b. Avoid drinking water so you won't put on water weight.
   c. Read up on proper nutrition and design a food plan for yourself.

7. **Drinking eight glasses of water a day is healthy because . . .**
   a. it helps the body metabolize fat and maintain muscle tone.
   b. it gives me something to do.
   c. it fills me up so I won't need any food.

8. **Walking is one of the best kinds of exercise because . . .**

   a. it is an aerobic exercise and provides the body with more oxygen.

   b. you can walk and get it over with, not having to do any other kind of exercise.

   c. you don't need special equipment, you can wear any old shoes.

9. **You realize you need to begin an exercise program. To get started you should . . .**

   a. jump right in, and run five miles the first day.

   b. start out gradually and increase your time to a maximum of four to five days/week.

   c. run in the morning, afternoon, and evening.

10. **In health class, the teacher presented a seminar on things you can do to take care of yourself through exercise, good nutrition, developing positive habits, and building your self-esteem. Your first thought was . . .**

    a. developing a plan for all-around fitness makes sense.

    b. I can take care of myself and feel good about myself if I control what I eat and make sure I don't put on any weight.

    c. what kind of a nerd would buy into this?

Answers, page 125

Where to Find Help

Academy for Eating Disorders (AED)
c/o Division of Adolescent Medicine
Montefiore Medical School
111 E. 210th St.
Bronx, NY 10467
(718) 920-6782

American Anorexia/Bulimia Association, Inc.
165 W. 46th Street, Ste. 1108
New York, NY 10036
(212) 575-6200

Anorexia Nervosa and Related Eating Disorders
(ANRED)
P.O. Box 5102
Eugene, OR 97405
(541) 344-1144

Association for the Health Enrichment for Large
People (AHELP)
P.O. Drawer C
Radford, VA 24143
(540) 951-3527

Food and Nutrition Information Center
National Agricultural Library
USDA
Room 304
Beltsville, MD 20705-2351
(301) 344-3719

International Association of Eating Disorders Professionals
123 NW 13th St.
Boca Raton, Florida 33432
(561) 338-6494

International Center for Sports Nutrition
502 S. 44th St.
Suite 3012
Omaha, NE 68015
(402) 559-5505

International Eating Disorders Organization (NEDO)
6655 S. Yale Ave.
Tulsa, OK 74136
(918) 481-4044

National Association of Anorexia Nervosa and Associated Disorders (ANAD)
P.O. Box 7
Highland Park, IL 60035
(847) 831-3438
ANAD will supply free materials and speakers to schools on eating disorders. They also have conducted the largest study in the country on the subject, involving 35,000 high school students.

National Association to Advance Fat Acceptance, Inc. (NAAFA)
P.O. Box 188620
Sacramento, CA 95818
(800) 442-1214 or (916) 558-6880, Monday–Thursday,
8:00 A.M.–4:00 P.M., Pacific time

National Center for Nutrition and Dietetics
The American Dietetic Association
216 W. Jackson Blvd., Suite 800
Chicago, IL 60606-5995
(312) 899-0040, ext. 4853

Overeater's Anonymous (OA)
World Services Office
P.O. Box 44020
Rio Rancho, NM 87124-4020
(505) 891-2664

Weight-Control Information Network
1 WIN WAY
Bethesda, MD 20892-3665
(301) 570-2177
WINNIDDK@aol.com

Chapter Notes

Chapter One

1. Allison, personal interview, July 1995.

2. Tim Allis, "Coping With a Consuming Obsession," *People Weekly*, January 31, 1994, p. 56.

3. Marilyn Lawrence, *The Anorexic Experience* (London: Women's Press, 1984), p. 41.

4. L. M. Mellin, "Responding to Disordered Eating in Children and Adolescents," *Nutrition News*, vol. 51 (1988), pp. 5–7. Cited in Centers for Disease Control Morbidity and Mortality Weekly Report, *JAMA*, vol. 266, no. 20, November 27, 1991, p. 2811.

5. Deb Rummel, Physical Management teacher, personal interview, June 1995.

6. Lauri Hargrove, health teacher, personal interview, June 1995.

7. Ellen Flax, "Class for Overweight Students at Illinois School Promotes Healthy Habits to Last a Lifetime," *Education Week*, vol. XI, no. 29, April 8, 1992, p. 6.

8. John P. Robinson and Geoffrey Godbey, *American Demographics*, vol. 15, issue 9, September 1993, p. 36.

9. Rummel.

10. Ibid.

11. "National Health and Nutrition Examination Survey III," cited in *Update*, July/August 1995, p. 1.

12. John H. Himes and William H. Dietz, "Guidelines for Overweight in Adolescents Preventive Services: Recommendations From an Expert Committee," *American Journal of Clinical Nutrition*, vol. 59, 1994, pp. 307–316.

13. Marissa, personal interview, July 1995.

14. *Science*, July 28, 1995. Cited in Paul Recer, "Studies Show Hormone Triggers Slimming Process," *Waukegan News-Sun*, p. C1.

15. Kari, personal interview, July 1995.

16. D. B. Herzog and P. M. Copeland, "Eating Disorders," *New England Journal of Medicine*, vol. 313, 1985, pp. 295–303, 668.

17. Mellin, pp. 5–7.

Chapter 2

1. Sandra H. Heater, *Am I Still Visible?* (White Hall, Va.: White Hall Books, 1983), p. 109.

2. *Eating Disorders*, National Institute of Mental Health pamphlet, p. 5.

3. Natalie, personal interview, August 1995.

4. Cherry Boone O'Neill, *Starving for Attention* (New York: Continuum, 1982), p. 41.

5. *Eating Disorders*, p. 11.

6. Nell, personal interview, August 1995.

7. *Eating and Exercise Disorders*, Anorexia Nervosa and Related Eating Disorders, Inc. pamphlet. This group is known as ANRED.

8. Vivian Meehan, R.N., founder of ANAD, personal interview, July 1995.

9. *Eating Disorders—Danger Signals and Treatment*, National Association of Anorexia and Associated Disorders, pamphlet.

10. *Eating Disorders: Decade of the Brain*, National Institute of Mental Health pamphlet, pp. 10–12.

Chapter 3

1. Marilyn Lawrence, *The Anorexic Experience* (London: The Women's Press, 1984), p. 47.

2. Marlene Boskind-White, Ph.D., and William C. White, Jr., Ph.D., *Bulimarexia* (New York: Norton, 1983), p. 20.

3. Karen S. Schneider, "Mission Impossible," *People*, June 3, 1996, p. 71.

4. Ibid., p. 70.

5. Marla Paul, *Chicago Tribune*, August 1995.

6. Barbara McFarland, Ed.D., and Tyeis Baker-Baumann, M.S., *Shame and Body Image: Culture and the Compulsive Eater* (Florida: Health Communications, 1990), p. 103.

7. Ibid., p. 91.

8. Ibid., p. 95.

9. Annie, personal interview, August 1995.

10. Boskind-White and White, pp. 83–85.

11. McFarland and Baker-Baumann, p. 90.

12. Jane Hirschmann and Carol Munter, "Let's Curb Our Appetite for Dieting," *Chicago Tribune*, January 19, 1997, Women's Tempo, p. 5.

13. Amy, personal interview, 1995.

Chapter 4

1. Marilyn Lawrence, *The Anorexic Experience* (London: The Women's Press, 1984), p. 48.

2. Ibid., p. 65.

3. Natalie, personal interview, August 1995.

4. Sheila MacLeod, *The Art of Starvation* (London: Virago, 1981), p. 65.

5. Katherine Byrne, *A Parent's Guide to Anorexia and Bulimia* (New York: Schocken Books, 1987), p. xiii.

Chapter 5

1. Natalie, personal interview, August 1995.

2. Sheila MacLeod, *The Art of Starvation* (London: Virago, 1981), p. 70.

3. Cathy Devlin, R.N., CEDS, dietician, personal interview, July 1995.

4. Julie, personal interview, July 1995.

5. Marilyn Lawrence, *The Anorexic Experience* (London: The Women's Press, 1984), p. 24.

6. MacLeod, p. 5.

7. Ibid., p. 66.

8. Erin, personal interview, July 1995.

9. Karen S. Schneider and Todd Gold, "A Brave New Song," *People*, June 19, 1995, p. 94.

10. Lawrence, p. 21.

11. Lillie Weiss, Ph.D., Melanie Katzman, Ph.D., and Sharlene Wolchik, Ph.D., *You Can't Have Your Cake and Eat It Too* (Saratoga, Calif.: R&E Publishers, 1986), p. 21.

12. Lisa Messenger, *Biting the Hand That Feeds Me* (Novato, Calif.: Arena Press, 1986), p. 145.

13. Nell, personal interview, August 1995.

14. Cherry Boone O'Neill, *Starving for Attention* (New York: Continuum, 1982), p. 15.

15. MacLeod, p. 22.

16. Erin.

17. MacLeod, pp. 51–53.

18. Nancy Thode, M.S.W., "Leaving Home: The Launching Stage of the Family Life Cycle," *American Anorexic/Bulimic Association Newsletter*, Fall 1993, p. 3.

19. Weiss, Katzman, and Wolchik, p. 7.

20. Ibid., p. 55.

Chapter 6

1. National Association of Anorexia and Associated Disorders, media page.

2. Quoted in Donna Alvarado, "Too Much of a Good Thing: When Exercise Becomes An Addiction," *Chicago Tribune*, August 22, 1990, pp. 12–13.

3. Ibid.

4. Nell, personal interview, August 24, 1995.

5. Erin, personal interview, July 1995.

6. Kathryn J. Zerbe, M.D., *Body Betrayed: Women, Eating Disorders, and Treatment* (Washington, D.C.: American Psychiatric Press, 1993), p. 348.

7. Nancy Logue, "Intensive Outpatient Treatment: Comparisons for Eating Disorders and Substance Abuse," *Addiction & Recovery*, September/October 1993, pp. 14–16.

8. Zerbe, p. 345.

Chapter 7

1. Allison, personal interview, August 1995.

2. Kari, personal interview, August 8, 1995.

3. Geneen Roth, *Breaking Free from Compulsive Eating* (New York: MacMillan Publishing Co., 1984).

4. Kathryn J. Zerbe, M.D., *Body Betrayed: Women, Eating Disorders, and Treatment* (Washington, D.C.: American Psychiatric Press, 1993), p. 286.

5. Ibid.

6. Ibid.

7. Zerbe, p. 287.

8. Jean P. Fisher and Bob Condor, "Health Officials Prod 'Couch Potatoes': Major Fitness Reports Says U.S. Isn't," *Chicago Tribune*, July 12, 1996.

9. Michelle Ingrassia, "The Body of the Beholder," *Newsweek*, April 24, 1995, p. 67.

10. Paula Lauer, "Why Just Do It? Here Are 50 Reasons to Help Keep You on Exercise Routine," *Waukegan News-Sun*, "On the Go" column, January 1, 1996.

11. "Walking," Heath Education Associates, Inc., Massachusetts, 1988, pamphlet.

12. Joy Berry, *Good Answers to Tough Questions About Weight Problems and Eating Disorders* (Chicago: Children's Press, 1990), pp. 16–17.

13. Lauerman, 1996 Council on Size and Weight Discrimination, Inc.

14. Karen S. Schneider, "Mission Impossible," *People*, June 3, 1996, p. 66.

Glossary

addiction—A dependency on a substance or activity. Major addictions involve drugs, alcohol, or excessive behavior with food.

amenorrhea—The absence of menstrual periods in a woman who would be expected to menstruate.

anorexia nervosa—The deliberate act of starving oneself in the pursuit of thinness. A characteristic of the anorexic is the compulsive use of exercise, laxatives, and/or diuretics. If not treated properly, anorexics can become malnourished and, in extreme cases, die.

antidepressant—A drug that alleviates depression, usually by energizing the person and chemically elevating the mood; Prozac, Elavil, and Paxil are some of the most commonly used antidepressants.

anxiety—A strong feeling of apprehension, as if something terrible were about to happen. This emotional state can become painful and result in feelings of panic that may cause physical symptoms.

assertive behavior—Expressing one's thoughts, feelings, and beliefs to others, as well as making needs and wishes known, rather than denying them.

behavior therapy—A type of psychotherapy that involves applying procedures such as modeling or reinforcing to help a person unlearn old behaviors and learn new ones.

binge-eating disorder—Eating large quantities of food in a short period of time, without purging. Includes strong feelings of low self-worth, guilt, shame and powerlessness. Food is used to soothe or distract the eater from pain. Also called compulsive overeating.

bingeing—Taking in large amounts of food in brief periods of time.

body image—Body image is connected with a person's self-image and has to do with how comfortable or satisfied a person feels about his or her size, shape, and/or appearance. It is often influenced by the values of one's family, peers, and the media.

body mass index (BMI)—A method of calculating body fat that combines height and weight.

bulimia/bulimia nervosa—Also called the "binge-purge syndrome." Sufferers alternately binge on large quantities of food, then purge the food by making themselves vomit or taking diuretics and/or laxatives. Bulimia is a mental disorder that usually affects young women in their 20s and 30s, as well as some men.

calorie—The unit of measurement of the energy-producing value of food.

compulsive overeating—The inability to control food intake. Overeaters often make repeated attempts to lose weight by dieting. Going up and down in weight can lead to medical problems such as diabetes or high blood pressure. Also called binge-eating disorder.

denial—Unconsciously refusing to accept some external stimulus or situation. This defense mechanism is adopted because it may be too painful for the person to recognize and accept reality.

depression—An emotional state marked by sadness and apprehension, feelings of worthlessness, and guilt. Someone who is depressed may withdraw from others, have trouble sleeping, and lose his/her appetite.

distorted thinking—Misrepresentation of reality or what is really happening.

eating disorder—An unhealthy pattern of food-related behavior based on a distorted self-image. Weight and dieting success are overly important to the person with an eating disorder, and her/his behavior toward food and eating often becomes rigid, repeated, and ritualistic. Someone with an eating disorder may constantly "feel fat," have a fear of becoming fat, or feel guilty when eating, yet continually fast, diet, or overeat.

identity crisis—A chaotic sense of self, particularly during adolescence. A person feels unwilling or unable to accept or adopt the role he believes is expected of him by society. An identity crisis often manifests itself by isolation, withdrawal, rebelliousness, negativity, or extremism.

leptin—A natural hormone that causes the bodies of obese rats to burn excess fat.

metabolism—Chemical changes in living cells by which energy is provided for vital processes and activities; the building up and destruction of protoplasm.

mood swings—Back-and-forth movement of a person's emotions and feelings, swinging between periods of elation and periods of depression.

obesity—Twenty percent or more above a healthy body weight range.

obsessive thinking—Persistent, unwanted, recurrent thoughts, often including severe brooding and doubting.

overweight—Weighing 20 percent more than the recommended weight for a person's height, age, and build.

psychiatrist—A medical doctor trained in the branch of medicine that deals with assessment and modifying of abnormal behavior. A medical doctor is able to prescribe medication but a psychologist cannot.

psychologist, clinical—A professional trained in research, assessment of behavior, psychological testing, and methods of psychotherapy who works with clients needing psychological guidance.

puberty—The period of growth when a young person's sexual organs start to develop, making him or her capable of reproducing sexually; usually occurs at fourteen years in boys, twelve years in girls.

rationalization—An unconscious defense mechanism in which irrational or unacceptable behavior, motives, or feelings are logically justified or made tolerable.

self-esteem—One's opinion of the value of oneself. A healthy self-esteem results from a match between what a person believes he or she is and what he or she would like to be.

set point—The level of calorie intake at which the body changes from its normal metabolism to a starvation-survival mode.

stress—Demanding or threatening events and the body's largely physical response to them.

Further Reading

Books

Berry, Joy. *Good Answers to Tough Questions About Weight Problems and Eating Disorders*. Chicago: Children's Press, 1990.

Boskind-White, Marlene, Ph.D., and William C. White, Jr., Ph.D. *Bulimarexia*. New York: Norton, 1983.

Brisman, Judith, Ph.D., Michele Siegel, Ph.D., and Margot Weinsel, M.S.W. *Surviving an Eating Disorder*. New York: Harper & Row, 1988.

Brownell, Kelly, and John Foreyt, eds. *Handbook of Eating Disorders: Physiology, Psychology and Treatment of Obesity, Anorexia and Bulimia*. New York: Basic Books, 1986.

Bruch, Hilde. *Eating Disorders: Obesity, Anorexia Nervosa and the Person Within*. New York: Basic Books, 1973.

———. *The Golden Cage*. Cambridge, Mass.: Harvard University Press, 1978.

Butler, Pamela. *Self-Assertion for Women*. New York: Harper & Row, 1981.

Byrne, Katherine. *A Parent's Guide to Anorexia and Bulimia*. New York: Shocken Books, 1987.

Davis, Martha, Ph.D., Elizabeth Robbins-Eshelman, M.S.W., and Matthew McKay, Ph.D. *The Relaxation and Stress-Reduction Workbook*. Oakland, Calif.: New Harbinger, 1982.

Garner, David, Ph.D., and Paul E. Garfinkel, M.D. *Handbook of Psychotherapy for Anorexia Nervosa and Bulimia*. New York: Guilford Press, 1985.

Heater, Sandra. *Am I Still Visible?* White Hall, Va.: White Hall Books, 1983.

Hollis, Judi, Ph.D. *Fat Is a Family Affair*. Center City, Minn.: Hazelden Foundation, 1985.

Jacobson, Edmund. *Progressive Relaxation*. Chicago: University of Chicago Press, Midway Reprint, 1974.

———. *You Must Relax*. New York: McGraw-Hill, 1978.

Johnson, Craig, Ph.D., and Mary E. Conners, Ph.D. *The Etiology and Treatment of Bulimia Nervosa*. New York: Basic Books, 1987.

Kolodny, Nancy J., M.A., M.S.W. *When Food's a Foe*. Boston, Mass.: Little, Brown, 1992.

Lawrence, Marilyn. *The Anorexic Experience*. London: The Women's Press, 1984.

Levenkron, Steven. *Treating and Overcoming Anorexia Nervosa*. New York: Scribner, 1982.

MacLeod, Sheila. *The Art of Starvation*. London: Virago, 1981.

McFarland, Barbara, Ed.D., and Tyeis Baker-Baumann, M.S. *Shame and Body Image: Culture and the Compulsive Eater*. Deerfield Beach, Fla.: Health Communications, 1990.

Messenger, Lisa. *Biting the Hand That Feeds Me*. Novato, Calif.: Arena Press, 1986.

Newbold, H. L. *Dr. Newbold's Revolutionary New Discoveries About Weight Loss*. New York: Signet, 1979.

O'Neill, Cherry Boone. *Starving for Attention*. New York: Continuum, 1982.

Pope, Harrison, G., Jr., M.D., and James Hudson, M.D. *New Hope for Binge Eaters*. New York: Harper & Row, 1984.

Roth, Geneen. *Feeding the Hungry Heart: The Experience of Compulsive Eating*. New York: Plume, 1982.

Sacker, Ira M., M.D., and Mark Zimmer, Ph.D. *Dying to Be Thin*. New York: Warner Books, 1987.

Sandbeck, Terence, Ph.D. *The Deadly Diet*. Oakland, Calif.: New Harbinger, 1986.

Satter, Ellyn. *How to Get Your Child to Eat . . . But Not Too Much*. Palo Alto, Calif.: Bull, 1987.

Schwartz, Mark F., Sc.D., and Leigh Cohn, M.A.T., eds. *Sexual Abuse and Eating Disorders: A Clinical Overview*. New York: Brunner/Mazel, 1996.

Smith, Manuel J. *When I Say No, I Feel Guilty*. New York: Dial Press, 1975.

Squire, Susan. *The Slender Balance*. New York: Putnam, 1983.

Stanlee, Phelps, and Nancy Austin. *The Assertive Woman*. San Luis Obispo, Calif.: Impact, 1975.

Valette, Brett E. *A Parent's Guide to Eating Disorders*. New York: Walker, 1988.

Vredevelt, Pam, and Joyce Whitman. *Walking a Thin Line*. Oregon: Muttnomah Press, 1985.

Weiss, Lillie, Ph.D., Melanie Katzman, Ph.D., and Sharlene Wolchik, Ph.D. *You Can't Have Your Cake and Eat It Too*. Saratoga, Calif.: R&E Publishers, 1986.

Wirtman, Judith. *Eating Your Way Through Life*. Lancaster, Calif.: Raven Press, 1979.

Zerbe, Kathryn J., M.D. *The Body Betrayed: Women, Eating Disorders, and Treatment*. Washington, D.C.: American Psychiatric Press, 1993.

Pamphlets

Go! Go! An Exercise Program for Healthy People. Chicago Heart Association pamphlet.

CMG Managed Health Care Criteria for Assessing Severity of Illness in Eating Disorder Patients. Preferred Health Care, 1990, Sec. VII.

Dietary Guidelines for Americans. U.S. Department of Agriculture, U.S. Department of Health and Human Services. Bulletin No. 232. Washington, D.C.: November 1990.

Eating and Exercise Disorders. Anorexia Nervosa and Related Eating Disorders (P.O. Box 5102, Eugene, OR 97405) pamphlet.

Eating Disorders. American Dietetic Association (216 W. Jackson Blvd., Suite 800, Chicago, IL 60606) pamphlet.

Hollis, Judi, Ph.D. *Accepting Powerlessness: The Food Obsession.* Minn.: Hazelden, 1984.

How Much Exercise Is Enough? LifeLines pamphlet. Fairfield, N.J.: Economics Press, 1983.

Levitt, John, Ph.D., and Catherine Cotter, A.C.S.W. *Dangerous Dieting: How It Can Lead to an Eating Disorder.* Pamphlet. Elk Grove Village, Ill.: Alexian Brothers Medical Center's Trauma/Eating Disorder Programs,

Methods of Voluntary Weight Loss and Control. National Institutes of Health, Technology Assessment Conference statement. March 30–April 1, 1992.

Shortchanging Girls, Shortchanging America. American Association of University Women report. Washington, D.C.: 1991.

Solberg, Eileen. *Physical Management Manual.* (P.O. Box 891, Billings, MT 59103; 406-252-4822).

When Image Becomes an Obsession, It's Time to Take a Closer Look! ANAD (Box 7, Highland Park, IL 60035) pamphlet.

Articles and Television Shows

Alvarado, Donna. "Too Much of a Good Thing: When Exercise Becomes an Addiction." *Chicago Tribune*, August 22, 1990, sec. 7, p. 13.

Casey, Kathryn. "We're Strong, Successful, in Control. So Why Can't We Stop Eating When We Want to Stop Eating? A Special Report on the Most Common Addiction of All." *Ladies Home Journal*, November 1992, pp. 187, 270–272.

Condor, Bob, and Jean P. Fisher. "Health Officials Prod 'Couch Potatoes.' Major Fitness Report Says U.S. Isn't." *Chicago Tribune*, July 12, 1996.

Davis, Bill, Ph.D., "Eating Disorders vs. Drug and Alcohol Addiction." *Addiction & Recovery*, September/October 1993, pp. 11–13.

Flax, Ellen, "Focus on Students." *Education Week*, April 1992.

Ford, Bob. "Spotlight Casts Cruel Shadows on Girls." (Book review of Joan Ryan's *Little Girls in Pretty Boxes: The Making and Breaking of Elite Gymnasts and Skaters*. New York: Doubleday, 1995.) *Chicago Tribune*, August 28, 1995, sec. 5, p. 5.

"Futility and Avoidance: Medical Professionals in the Treatment of Obesity." *JAMA*, vol. 269, no. 16, April 28, 1993, pp. 2132–2133.

Hirschmann, Jane, and Carol Munter. "Let's Curb Our Appetite for Dieting." *Chicago Tribune*, January 19, 1997, p. 5.

Lauerman, Connie. "Making Fun of Fat People May Be 'the Last Safe Prejudice,' and Many Think It's Got to Go." *Chicago Tribune*, July 1, 1996, pp. 1, 5.

Leland, John, et al. "The Body Impolitic: Fashion and Its Critics Sell the Same Stereotypes." *Newsweek*, June 17, 1996, p. 66.

Logue, Nancy, Ph.D. "Intensive Outpatient Treatment: Comparisons for Eating Disorders and Substance Abuse." *Addiction & Recovery*, September/October 1993, pp. 14–16.

Price, James H., Sharon M. Desmond, Elizabeth Ruppert, and Peg J. Sauder. "Parents' Perceptions of Childhood Obesity and the Role of Schools." *Journal of Health Education*, vol. 23, no.1, January/February 1992, pp. 32–37.

Recer, Paul. "Studies Show Hormone Triggers Slimming Process." *Waukegan News Sun*, July 28, 1995.

Ross, Julia, M.A., M.F.C.C. "Food Addiction: A New Look at the Nature of Craving." *Addiction & Recovery*, September/October 1993, pp. 17–19.

Scherr, Lynn, narrator. "The Hunger Inside." *20/20*, ABC News, December 1994.

Schneider, Karen, and Todd Gold. "A Brave New Song." *People*, June 19, 1995.

Schneider, Karen, et al. "Mission Impossible." *People*, June 3, 1996.

Smith, Marya. "Mentor." *Chicago Tribune*, July 23, 1995.

Springman, Karen, and Allison Samuels. "The Body of the Beholder." *Newsweek*, April 24, 1995, pp. 66–67.

Thode, Nancy, M.S.W. "Leaving Home: The Launching Stage of the Family Life Cycle." *American Anorexic/Bulimic Association Newsletter* (Greenwich, Conn.: Williams Center for Eating Disorders), 1995, p. 3.

Update, newsletter of the American Alliance for Health, Physical Education, Recreation and Dance, July/August 1995.

Watson, Traci, and Corinna Wu. "Are You Too Fat?" *U.S. News & World Report*, January 9, 1996, pp. 52–53, 56, 58–61.

Yates, Alayne, M.D. "Bulimia as a Complicating Factor in Men." *Addiction & Recovery*, September/October 1993, p. 20.

Answer Key

Test Your Weight I.Q., page 17
Answers: 1. b, 2. a, 3. b, 4. c, 5. a, 6. c, 7. a, 8. c, 9. c, 10. b, 11. b.

Eating "Secrets," page 33
Answers: 1. b, 2. a, 3. c, 4. b, 5. a, 6. b, 7. b, 8. c, 9. b, 10. a

Dying to Be Thin, page 48
Answers: 1. b, 2. b, 3. b, 4. b, 5. a, 6. b, 7. b, 8. a, 9. a, 10. c.

Knowing Yourself, page 59
Answers: 1. c, 2. b, 3. c, 4. c, 5. a, 6. c, 7. b, 8. c

Controlled by Food, page 87
Answers: 1. a, 2. a, 3. c, 4. b, 5. a, 6. c, 7. c, 8. a, 9. c, 10. a

Are You Fit?, page 102
Answers: 1. a, 2. a, 3. b, 4. b, 5. a, 6. c, 7. a, 8. a, 9. b, 10. a

— If you got seven or more correct for each quiz, you are probably quite weight-wise.
— If you got between four and six correct, you know some things about healthy weight management but need to learn more.
— If you got less than four correct, you may be following some unhealthy weight management practices that may create problems for you in the future.

Index